PROFESSIONALISM IN THE REAL WORLD

LESSONS FOR THE EFFECTIVE ADVOCATE

PROFESSIONALISM IN THE REAL WORLD

LESSONS FOR THE EFFECTIVE ADVOCATE

Lisa Penland
Melissa H. Weresh

NATIONAL INSTITUTE FOR TRIAL ADVOCACY

Reprint Permission
National Institute for Trial Advocacy
361 Centennial Parkway, Suite 220
Louisville, CO 80027
Phone: (800) 225-6482
Fax: (720) 890-7069
E-mail: permissions@nita.org

Library of Congress Cataloging-in-Publication Data
Penland, Lisa.
    Professionalism in the real world : lessons for the effective advocate / Lisa Penland, Melissa H. Weresh.
        p. cm.

    ISBN 978-1-60156-057-5
    1. Legal ethics--United States. I. Weresh, Melissa H. II. Title.
    KF306.P458 2009
    174'.30973--dc22
                        2009004505

ISBN 978-1-60156-057-5

FBA 1057

12 11 10 09   10 9 8 7 6 5 4 3 2 1

Printed in the United States of America

CONTENTS

ACKNOWLEDGMENTS

We would like to thank Drake University Law School for its support of this project. Research assistants Brant Leonard, Zack Brost, and Seth Delutri provided valuable research and editorial assistance. We are also indebted to members of the Drake Law Library faculty, particularly Sue Lerdal, Karen Wallace, and Brian Fodrey. Finally, we would like to thank our families for their support.

The authors acknowledge the permissions kindly granted to reproduce excerpts from the materials indicated below:

ABA *Model Rules of Professional Conduct*, 2008 Edition. Copyright © 2008 by the American Bar Association. Reprinted with permission. Copies of ABA *Model Rules of Professional Conduct*, 2008 Edition, are available from Service Center, American Bar Association, 321 North Clark Street, Chicago, IL 60654, 1-800-285-2221.

ABA *Formal Ethics Opinion, 92-363* 1992 Edition. Copyright © 1992 by the American Bar Association. Reprinted with permission. Copies of *ABA Formal Ethics Opinion*, 1992 Edition, are available from Service Center, American Bar Association, 321 North Clark Street, Chicago, IL 60654, 1-800-285-2221.

ABA *Formal Ethics Opinion*, 92-383 1992 Edition. Copyright © 1992 by the American Bar Association. Reprinted with permission. Copies of *ABA Formal Ethics Opinion*, 1992 Edition, are available from Service Center, American Bar Association, 321 North Clark Street, Chicago, IL 60654, 1-800-285-2221.

ABA *Formal Ethics Opinion*, DR 7-105A 2007 Edition. Copyright © 2007 by the American Bar Association. Reprinted with permission. Copies of *ABA Formal Ethics Opinion*, 1992 Edition, are available from Service Center, American Bar Association, 321 North Clark Street, Chicago, IL 60654, 1-800-285-2221.

R.J. Gerber, *Victory vs. Truth: The Adversary System and Its Ethics*, 19 ARIZ. ST. L.J. 3, 15–6 (1987).

ETHICAL AND PROFESSIONAL SOURCES OF INFLUENCE

This book focuses on ethical and professional communication in advocacy. Specifically, it will illustrate how to communicate professionally in different advocacy settings. Our first consideration is what sources should influence our behavior and communication as lawyers in the context of ethics and professionalism. There are three sources that we draw upon to maintain an ethical, professional practice. These include rules, including rules of ethics as well as procedural rules that impose ethical and professional obligations; conventions of professionalism, either formally embodied in professionalism codes or more informally imposed by the expectations of peers; and a sense of personal character or integrity. Before focusing on specific considerations applicable to representation, it is important to understand how the ethical and professional behavior of lawyers is monitored.

Sources of ethical practice

The most obvious influence in terms of ethical and professional communication in law practice is the code of ethical rules that formally govern the profession. Upon admission to the bar in a particular jurisdiction, a lawyer becomes subject to the jurisdiction's rules of professional responsibility. Once subject to those rules, lawyers are self-regulating. As noted in the American Law Institute's Restatement of the Law Governing Lawyers, "[u]pon admission to the bar of any jurisdiction, a person becomes a lawyer and is subject to applicable law governing such matters as professional discipline, procedure and evidence, civil remedies, and criminal sanctions."[1] Further, the Preamble to the ABA Model Rules of Professional Conduct explains:

> The legal profession is largely self-governing. Although other professions also have been granted powers of self-government, the legal profession is unique in this respect because of the close relationship between the profession and the processes of government and law enforcement.

So, when a lawyer becomes admitted to the bar in a particular state, she becomes regulated by the ethics rules adopted by that state. She will be subject not only to the rules of ethics applicable in her jurisdiction, but also to procedural rules that govern the format and substance of her communications and may impose additional ethical requirements. Moreover, her professional reputation will be based upon her ability

---

1. Restatement (Third) of the Law Governing Lawyers § 1 (2000).

to recognize and adhere to the expectations of professionalism in that legal community. Some of those expectations may be codified in the form of a code or oath of professionalism, while others are merely informal conventions within the legal community. Finally, her own sense of character or integrity will influence how she communicates in practice.

I. ETHICAL AND PROCEDURAL RULES

Many local rules of procedure impose ethical obligations on lawyers as they engage in professional communication. For example, Federal Rule of Civil Procedure 11 prohibits a lawyer from filing a frivolous claim. This prohibition obligates the lawyer to effectively research and investigate a client matter to ensure that there is a good-faith basis in law and fact to support the claim. It implicitly obligates a lawyer to represent the client truthfully. In addition, lawyers are subject to ethical rules by virtue of their admission to the bar in a particular state. Most states have adopted some form of the American Bar Association Model Rules of Professional Conduct. With regard to ethical rules, this book focuses on those rules relating to an attorney's communications in her representational function. These will be discussed in greater detail and as they apply in later chapters. However, there are a number of overarching concepts that govern ethical attorney behavior in general and, therefore, guide an attorney's communications in the practice of law.

A. Competence

The rule regarding an attorney's competence governs her behavior in all legal representation. The Preamble to the Model Rules specifically identifies competence as governing all professional functions of a lawyer. In addition, the first Model Rule of Professional Conduct, Rule 1.1, is directed to competence. That this rule is first implies its importance. The rule notes that "[c]ompetent representation requires the legal knowledge, skill, thoroughness and preparation reasonably necessary for the representation." The relationship between competence and an attorney's communication with other members of the bar, judges, clients, and other persons in the course of legal representation is not necessarily direct; rather, the requirement of competence is a comprehensive principle that influences all attorney communication. The comments to this rule require that a lawyer have adequate legal knowledge and skill, be thorough and prepared, and comply with continuing legal education requirements in order to remain abreast of changes in the law to ensure continuing competence. Thus, the attorney's communications must be informed by the standard of competence and must evidence the attorney's competence.

B. Diligence and Timeliness

The Preamble to the Model Rules states that "[i]n all professional functions a lawyer should be competent, prompt and diligent." In addition to competence, diligence and timeliness are overarching principles governing attorney behavior in general, and, in turn, attorney communications with others. While timeliness and diligence are themes throughout the Model Rules, they are emphasized in Model Rule of Professional Conduct 1.3, which provides: "A lawyer shall act with reasonable diligence and promptness in representing a client." Thus, this rule requires timely and diligent communication with clients.

The Rules directly address timeliness and diligence in relation to attorneys' communications during representation. For example, Model Rule of Professional Conduct 1.4 requires prompt and diligent communication with clients on certain matters, such as when informed consent must be obtained. Other rules, such as Model Rule of Professional Conduct 1.8, address diligent disclosure of conflicts of interests. In sum, the concepts of diligence and timeliness apply to all attorney communications and, in some instances, are addressed in the context of specific types of communications.

C. Communication with Clients

Although the ethics rules address ethical communication toward a variety of audiences, including opposing parties and the court, the Preamble specifically emphasizes an attorney's obligation to "maintain communication with a client concerning the representation." As noted earlier, Rule 1.4 of the Model Rules specifically addresses an attorney's communications with her client, and Model Rule of Professional Conduct 1.5 specifically addresses communication of fee arrangements. Indeed, there is extensive coverage relating to the communication between attorney and client throughout the Rules. This makes it clear that conforming to the rules of ethics when communicating with clients is paramount to proper representation.

D. Fairness

Fairness is another principle that governs representational attorney communications. For example, Model Rule of Professional Conduct 4.2 addresses the obligation of fairness in terms of communicating with someone who is represented by counsel. This rule prohibits a lawyer from communicating with a person represented by counsel "unless the lawyer has the consent of the other lawyer or is authorized to do so by law or a court order." This rule essentially prohibits unfair communication. Other rules require an attorney to reveal her representation to unrepresented persons and prohibit ex parte communication with the court. There are additional examples of the fairness obligation throughout the rules. But it is most important for the attorney to simply keep fairness in mind in her representational communications.

E. Truthfulness

The Model Rules also impose an obligation of truthfulness in communicating with the client, opposing parties, the court, and others. Like fairness, the obligation of truthfulness is not directly addressed in the Preamble, but it is a continuing theme throughout the rules. For example, Model Rule of Professional Conduct 2.1 requires a lawyer to "render candid advice." According to the rule, candid advice includes reference not only to the law, but also to "moral, economic, social and political factors, that may be relevant to the client's situation." The comments to this rule make it clear that the lawyer has an ethical obligation to be frank with the client, even when the lawyer's advice may be unpleasant or disappointing to the client.

In addition, a lawyer has an explicit obligation of candor toward the tribunal, which is set forth in Model Rule of Professional Conduct 3.3. Model Rule of Professional Conduct 4.1 addresses a lawyer's obligation with respect to truthfulness in statements to others. These are just a few examples of the underlying principle of truthfulness in attorney representational communications.

F. Confidentiality

The Preamble to the Model Rules states that "[a] lawyer should keep in confidence information relating to the representation of the client except so far as disclosure is required or permitted by the Rules of Professional Conduct or other law." Confidentiality, tempered by truthfulness and disclosure, is another overarching principle of the rules of ethics.

As will be more fully discussed in the following chapters, a lawyer must preserve the confidentiality of client information when communicating in the advocacy setting. As you communicate verbally, either in person or by phone; electronically via e-mail, internet, and facsimile; and in hardcopy, the duty to maintain confidences is implicated.

II. PROFESSIONALISM STANDARDS

As noted, in addition to the rules of ethics that govern lawyers as members of the bar, lawyers may also be subject to formal codes or oaths of professionalism adopted by state or local bar associations. These codes typically address professionalism issues such as courtesy and civility in the practice of law. In addition to codes of professionalism, rules of procedure impose obligations of professionalism. For example, compliance with local rules of court that address the format of certain documents is a manifestation of the professionalism of an advocate. Further, as with any professional community, there are expectations of professionalism that are informal. This concept is recognized in the Preamble to the Model Code of Professional Rules, which notes that "a lawyer is also guided by . . . the approbation of professional peers."

With regard to communications in the advocacy setting, conventions of professionalism, whether memorialized in a code or informally expected by peers, should influence the lawyer to behave courteously, respectfully, politely, and in a dignified manner. In addition to preserving your reputation, this type of behavior is beneficial to your effectiveness as an advocate. Granting an extension request where such extension has no adverse impact on the client is likely to result in similarly fair and favorable treatment to the advocate. Responding to an outraged opposing counsel with dignity and courtesy creates a favorable impression to the court and to your clients. In short, what goes around comes around. If you want to be treated kindly and fairly in law practice, make it a practice to treat others with kindness and fairness.

III. Personal Integrity

Your communications as a lawyer are not only guided by ethical rules and considerations of professionalism, but also by personal integrity and character. Interestingly, the Preamble to the Model Rules gives credence to this notion in stating that while "many of a lawyer's professional responsibilities are prescribed in the Rules of Professional Conduct" and in the law, "a lawyer is also guided by personal conscience . . ."

Your personal integrity has been formed throughout your life. As a lawyer, however, your professional reputation has an enormous impact on your effectiveness as an advocate. When you think of the attributes of good character or integrity that you admire in your friends and professional peers, apply those to your own professional discourse. Honesty, fairness, trustworthiness, and civility are all aspects of integrity that should influence you as you make choices in professional communication.

IV. Relationship between These Sources and Legal Communication

This manual has been designed to make lawyers more aware of how ethical rules and expectations of professionalism should influence their communications. You should note that you will likely practice with lawyers of all ages and from a variety of backgrounds. Lawyers from different generations may have different expectations about the degree of formality associated with certain communicative settings. For example, older lawyers may feel that e-mail is an inappropriate form of communication for certain legal issues while younger lawyers, who have long relied on electronic communication, may disagree. While there may be some legitimate disagreement in this respect, all lawyers must recognize that the rules of ethics relating to communication apply to all lawyers. Notions of professionalism may differ somewhat between lawyers, but we have outlined some of the basic considerations all lawyers should reflect upon as they engage in professional communication. Our hope is that this manual reinforces those expectations of professionalism that not only distinguish lawyers as members of a respected profession, but also enable lawyers to maintain a more effective, gratifying practice.

2

GENERAL CONSIDERATIONS

In Chapter 1, the sources that influence professionalism in the legal profession were identified. These sources of influence give rise to a variety of general considerations that impact a lawyer's professionalism in his communication. Ultimately, maintaining professionalism in your communication means not only conveying your trustworthiness to your recipient, but also your respect of others. This chapter will identify and discuss general considerations that apply to all forms of communication, as well as those within each type of communication. This chapter also provides some guidelines for communication with potential clients and advertising. Later chapters will more narrowly address specific considerations that arise in the context of particular practice settings.

I. GENERAL CONSIDERATIONS APPLICABLE TO ALL COMMUNICATION

There are several factors that will impact the professional presentation of a lawyer's communication, regardless of whether that communication is hard-copy, electronic, telephonic, or in-person. The key to determining how to effectively present a communication in a professional manner is to focus on clearly relaying the material to the recipient. By respecting the purpose—providing your recipient with information in a way that the recipient easily understands it—the lawyer treats the recipient in a respectful and professional manner.

A. Choosing the Method of Communication

Choosing the method of communication is the first focus of professionalism. Various factors should impact a lawyer's choice of communication, including audience, the type of information that the lawyer wants to relay to the recipient, time constraints, and the response expected as a result of the communication.

Clearly, audience is a key component of determining what method of communication you will use. Is your audience a twenty-something client who checks her e-mail daily, if not hourly, and is not only well-versed in how to use electronic communication, but prefers it? In that case, choosing an electronic communication demonstrates respect for the recipient's communication preferences and abilities. On the other hand, is your recipient an older individual from the boomer generation who only infrequently checks his e-mail? In that case, choosing electronic communication may convey disrespect for the recipient. Regardless of the age of your audience, determine his preference and communicate accordingly. If your audience is a person or entity having authority, such as a judge, a formal letter is often a better choice of communication. You should also consider whether you have some implicit or explicit communicative arrangement with the recipient. In other words, do prior agreements or past practice with the recipient suggest a particular format? Or are there applicable ethical or local court rules that require you to communicate with this particular recipient in a certain way?

Audience is clearly an important factor in determining what type of communication you will use. However, equally important is the substance of the communication. Is the information a formal transmittal, such as a client advice letter? In that case, a hard-copy letter is a better selection. Is the substance of the communication a brief inquiry? Perhaps, then, a quick telephone call or e-mail is more appropriate. If the substance of your communication is to allocate duties between yourself and another attorney in your firm, a face-to-face communication with a follow-up e-mail may be appropriate. Is the substance of your communication one that you want to memorialize in writing in order to have some sort of record of the communication? Is the substance of your communication emotional? At times, person-to-person or telephone communication is better when the substance is emotional. For example, are you going to tell a family law client that his ex-wife is going to attempt to prevent him from seeing his children? In such case, telephone the client and follow up the telephone call with a more formal hard-copy letter outlining your legal advice on the matter. The question to ask is what is the most effective method to deliver the information?

Time constraints are another significant factor in choosing the method of communication. While an advice letter is generally the method preferred for delivering legal advice to a client, there may be times when the client needs the information more quickly than can be provided by using a hard-copy letter. In that case, a telephone call or e-mail, with a follow-up formal letter, will be a more appropriate choice. A less formal method of communication or one that is not the "preferred" method of your audience may sometimes be necessary to deliver information in a timely manner.

A final consideration is the type of response you would like to receive. If an electronic or telephonic response to the initial communication is unacceptable, then it is probably also an unacceptable method of conveying the initial communication. As you communicate in law practice, you will want to consider the type of response your communication encourages. The response may not only suggest the method for your initial communication but may also require you to think about the content of that communication and how to express your expectations for their response. Again, when dealing with recipients who may have different expectations with respect to the method of communication you should be clear on your preferred method of response.

In sum, the first aspect of garnering respect from your recipients is to select a method of communication that—in light of the audience, the substance, the time constraints, and the desired type of response—conveys a respect for the recipient by choosing the best delivery method. Additional considerations include whether there are applicable ethical or court rules that impact the method of communication.

B. Know Your Audience

Law firms today are populated with employees spanning three, and possibly four, generations. Reports show that younger lawyers from Generation X (born

---

Cautionary Tale

As reported in the ABA Journal, Law News Now, "[t]he generational divide is playing out in law firm fashion wars, with younger lawyers favoring business casual and even yoga pants and older lawyers tending to wear more traditional business attire."[1] Similarly, the Wall Street Journal reported that some associates who fail to adhere to expectations regarding workplace attire risk disapproval and—worse— career setbacks.[2] In fact, the newspaper reported "When it came time to pick a point person for a plum assignment at Manatt, Phelps & Phillips recently, the New York law firm chose 'a polished, professional-looking associate' over a 'brilliant' and experienced associate who had been counseled, to no avail, to improve his grooming and attire, says Renee Brissette, a partner at the firm." Ugg boots worn by younger associates became a source of consternation at law firm Cadwalader Wickersham & Taft. Finally, at Winston and Strawn, the firm hired a personal shopper from a department store to give advice to young associates. An etiquette consultant hired by the firm noted that "many members of the so-called millennial generation have never been schooled in the traditions that previous generations learned at their parents' knees. Yet these 20-somethings are still being evaluated by old-school bosses and clients. Many members of this generation not only 'don't own a watch—they've never owned a watch,' says Ms. Neels. In many white-collar professions, an expensive watch signals success, while a cool cell phone or iPod, though it tells time, signals hipness."

---

1. Debra Cassens Weiss, *'Abysmal' Associate Attire Leads to Fashion Counseling*, ABA Journal, Law News Now, Jan. 31, 2008, available at www.abajournal.com/news/law_firms_offer_clothes_counseling_after_associates_casual_dress_irks_partn/.

2. Christina Brinkley, *Law Without Suits: New Hires Flout Tradition*, The Wall Street Journal, Jan. 31, 2008, available at http://online.wsj.com/article/SB120175142140831193.html?mod=home_law_more_news.

1964 to 1981) and the Millenial Generation (born 1981 to 1995) have vastly different expectations than Boomers (born 1946 to 1963) and the Silent Generation (born 1920 to 1945) about the degree of formality associated with law practice, and have different ideas about how hierarchies should function in the law firm setting. For example, younger lawyers tend to be more comfortable with "dress down" days than older lawyers. They also tend to approach electronic communication such as e-mail, text messaging, and social networking more casually and informally. It is clear that all lawyers are subject to the same ethical rules and, where applicable within jurisdictions, to the same formal professionalism codes. However, with respect to more informal expectations about professionalism, these differing expectations can result in perceived lapses in professionalism. Therefore, it is recommended that younger lawyers in particular "know their audience" and familiarize themselves with the expectations of other lawyers and judges in their community about the degree of formality expected in law practice.

C. Planning Your Communication

While some face-to-face communication is so informal as to not require planning, most communication in a professional setting should be carefully crafted to achieve a particular purpose. What better way to show respect for the recipient and the process of communication than to spend some time thinking about how and what you will communicate. Clearly, determining the most effective method of communication is one aspect of planning your communication. Other elements of planning require the practitioner to identify the purpose of the communication, to conduct an adequate investigation and inquiry before beginning the communication, and to anticipate the recipient's responses and needs. Determine the purpose of your communication in order to quickly convey that purpose to the recipient. Are you calling to obtain information? Let the recipient of the telephone call know that at the beginning of the conversation. Before picking up the telephone or sitting down to write, be sure that you have conducted an adequate investigation. That is, make sure that you have all of the information necessary to carry out the purpose of the communication. An attorney should not expect the recipient of her communication to provide information that she could find herself. If helpful to the recipient, and it is often is, provide contextual information to them along with the purpose of the communication to set the framework for your communication. Finally, anticipate the needs and responses of your recipient that will arise from the communication. Will your recipient need time to respond? Will your recipient need direction on how to respond? Will your recipient have an emotional response to the communication? Anticipate the responses and needs of your recipient and, to the extent possible, have in mind a plan that takes those needs and responses into account.

D. Watch Your Tone

Tone of voice is easy to detect, but difficult to define. When we warn our children against using that "tone of voice," they often defend themselves by pointing to the literal words of the communication, which, absent the tone of voice, are often innocuous. That defense does not work for them, and it will not work for the lawyer who uses sarcasm or a disrespectful tone in his communication in the practice of law. These negative tones do nothing to make the communication more effective, and most often the recipient will perceive (correctly) the negative tone as a disrespectful communication. In addition, sarcasm in written form often makes the communication less clear. Moreover, many codes of professionalism used by state and local bar associations specifically prohibit disrespect and incivility in legal communications. Thus, a negative tone, such as sarcasm or disrespect, should not merely be avoided in communicating in the practice of law; it should never be used.

While a lawyer should absolutely not use sarcasm or negative tones, she is forewarned to generally *avoid* humor and discussion of personal matters in business settings. While humor can be used to relieve tension, it can also lead to misunderstandings. Written humor, and irony in particular, may be misunderstood. If professionalism is shown through respect for the communication and the recipient, anything that makes the communication more difficult to understand undermines the appearance of professionalism. Further, humor is often at the expense of a particular group or person. A "dumb blond" joke is not so funny to the blond president of the company that you represent. Humor not only is often at the expense of a group, but it can easily slide into sexism and racism, which are not only inappropriate and disrespectful, but could also lead to legal repercussions.

Avoid discussing personal matters in all professional communications. While the attorney who represents the opposing party may be a close friend of yours, it is inappropriate to discuss personal matters with that attorney in a professional setting. Similarly, e-mails that discuss personal matters should be generally avoided in law practice. As a general rule, use home e-mail to plan social activities. Discussing personal matters with other lawyers in the presence of clients may appear disrespectful of the client's legal matter as well as the legal process. Commenting on the appearance of others is inappropriate as well.

This caveat seems to be self-evident, but it is so important that it bears saying: your professionalism is undermined by swearing or using foul language in a professional setting. While in some social, and even business, circles, swearing, foul language, and coarse dialogue are accepted, you cannot be assured that every person with whom you are orally communicating is accepting of such language. Further, oral communication may be formally "on the record," or less formally "on the record." A party to a communication is entitled to record it. Because an oral communication could be informally or formally recorded for future recipients and because written communication is always "on the record," whether officially or unofficially, the practicing lawyer cannot be assured how the communication will be received by future recipients. Surely, then, a professional should not swear or use foul or coarse language in conducting her practice.

The Nixon Tapes[3]

There are 3700 hours of telephone conversations that former President Nixon ordered secretly taped. As noted by Kyle O'Connor, an intern at the Miller Center of Public Affairs who helped transcribe the telephone conversations, "I was expecting the same dry, rehearsed policy-speak that is the norm . . . Instead, I found myself listening to the 37th president swear, rant, joke and preen . . . ."

E. Be Truthful

Under the Model Rules of Professional Conduct, an attorney has an ethical obligation to be truthful to the court, his client, and to third persons as well. The integrity of the attorney and the appearance of professionalism are undermined by engaging in deception and lying. While an attorney may, at times, be prohibited from disclosing information related to his representation, he must make every effort to be as forthright and honest as possible. The people who communicate with lawyers must be able to rely upon their honesty and integrity.

F. Keep Confidences (and More) Confidential

While an attorney has an ethical obligation to keep the client's information related to representation confidential, this is not the only ethical consideration that should drive the attorney in this respect. First, an attorney's trustworthiness and credibility and, in turn, her professionalism, are gravely undermined when the attorney discloses her client's confidences. Further, the attorney's trustworthiness and credibility are damaged not only by revealing client information that is technically confidential, but also by revealing information about the client that, while perhaps not confidential, would be considered personal by the client. The attorney's professionalism is not only undermined in the eyes of the client, but in the eyes of those persons with whom the attorney shares the confidential or personal information. Thus, in all communications, you should refrain from revealing confidential or personal information about your client.

---

3. Kyle O'Connor, *Last Look History Lesson*, UNIV. OF VA. ARTS AND SCI. MAGAZINE, Aug. 14, 2007 *available at* http://www.magazine.clas.virginia.edu/x11352.xml.

General Considerations

1. Choose the method of communication.

   • Who is your audience?

   • What method does your audience prefer?

   • Is the communication formal or informal?

   • Do you want a record of the communication?

   • Are there time constraints?

   • What is your preferred type of response?

2. Plan your communication.

   • Identify your purpose.

   • Investigate and research.

   • Anticipate your recipient's needs.

3. Watch your tone.

   • Don't use sarcasm or negative tone.

   • Avoid humor and personal matters.

   • Don't swear or use foul language.

4. Be truthful.

5. Keep confidences confidential.

II. GENERAL CONSIDERATIONS FOR WRITTEN COMMUNICATION

In addition to general considerations that a lawyer must be aware of with respect to all communications, there are also standards applicable specifically to written communications. While hard-copy communications are distinguishable from electronic communications, both are written forms of communication, and certain professionalism considerations apply to all written communications. Additionally, there are special confidentiality issues related to e-mail and fax communications.

A. Firm Names and Letterheads

A number of the rules relating to communication of attorney advertising and solicitation are discussed below in Section G. Because, however, the ethical rules related to firm names and letterheads go beyond the scope of advertising and solicitation, they are dealt with in this section. A firm name might appear in any type of written communication, be it a letterhead, a Web site, an e-mail communication, a sign, or otherwise. Thus, the practicing attorney should be certain that any time the firm name or letterhead appears it conforms to these rules.

According to Model Rule of Professional Conduct 7.5, a firm name or letterhead may not make a false or misleading communication about the lawyer or the lawyer's services. The rule allows for the use of a trade name so long as the use of such a trade name does not "imply a connection with a governmental agency or with a public or charitable legal services organization . . . ." So what is allowed? Comment 1 to the rule indicates that

1. "A firm name may be designated by the names of all or some of its members."

2. "A firm name may be designated by . . . the names of deceased members where there has been a continuing succession in the firm's identity."

3. "A firm name may be designated by . . . a trade name" so long as it is not misleading.

4. A firm name may also "be designated by a distinctive website address or comparable professional designation."

5. You may not "use the name of a lawyer not associated with the firm or a predecessor of the firm, or the name of a nonlawyer."[4]

The rule on firm names allows for the use of a single firm name in multiple jurisdictions, but requires that any jurisdictional limits on the lawyers' practice be identified. Also, the rule prohibits the use of a lawyer's name on letterhead if the lawyer holds public office and is not actively practicing law with the firm. Finally, the rule prohibits lawyers from representing a relationship with a firm unless that representation is true.

B. Pay Attention to Structure

An important concept of communicating is presenting the written communication in a manner in which the recipient can easily understand it. Providing your reader with a familiar and clear structure will ease his understanding. While many legal documents require a very specific structure, some general structural guidelines

---

4. MODEL RULES OF PROF'L CONDUCT R. 7.5 cmt. 1 (2008).

to keep in mind when communicating in writing are length, large-scale structure, and small-scale structure.

Every written communication should be structured to be only as long as necessary to communicate its contents. If you are writing a formal document that you will file with the court, do not view court rules setting page limitations as page requirements. If you can complete the communication in fewer pages than allowed, you should do so. Be particularly cognizant of length in e-mail communications, which, as a general rule, should be brief.

Every written communication should have a large-scale structure that can be outlined. If you are unable to outline your communication, it is doubtful that you have communicated in an effective and professional way. Where helpful or necessary, insert the headings and subheadings of your outline to assist the reader in maneuvering through your communication.

Finally, and closely related to length and large-scale structure, is small-scale structure. Have you used topic sentences for each paragraph? Have you provided your reader with transitions between paragraphs? Do the transitions make sense? Does one thought logically follow another? Have you used conclusions to communicate your ultimate opinion or thoughts on a particular topic?

Use large-scale structure to marshal your communication in a logical way. Edit to shorten where you are able or combine thoughts into a specific area of your communication. Finally, use transitions, topic sentences, and conclusions to present your communications to the recipient in a logically progressive manner.

C. Seek Clarity, Avoid Ambiguity

Keeping in mind that professionalism requires a reader-focused orientation, the question then becomes what writing conventions must a lawyer follow to communicate clearly and unambiguously? The professional must pay attention to several clarity guidelines, beginning with attention to grammar, punctuation, and capitalization. While outlining the rules of grammar, punctuation, and capitalization is beyond the scope of this text, we cannot express how important it is to follow these rules. First, failure to meet expectations about basic writing proficiencies will seriously undermine your credibility with the reader. Given that you are a trained professional with advanced education, your recipients expect you to use correct grammar, punctuation, and capitalization. If you do not, at best you will give the appearance of being a sloppy lawyer, but, at worst, a lawyer who does not know these rules. If you do not know the simple writing rules shared by most professionals, your clients, opponents, colleagues, employers, and judges will wonder whether you lack competency in the practice of law as well. However, not only do you lose credibility by failing to adhere to proper grammar, punctuation, and capitalization, you also make your communications more difficult to understand. The purpose of such rules is to create uniformity in communications so that recipients are able to understand them. By failing to adhere to simple grammar, punctuation, and capital-ization rules, your professionalism is undermined by your inability to communicate effectively.

There are other clarity considerations that may be viewed as guidelines, rather than rules. Employing these guidelines will increase the clarity of your communi-cation, making it more effective. In addition, the professional appearance of your communication will be enhanced by following these guidelines.

Your writing will be clearer if you avoid using acronyms. While some acronyms have been incorporated into our language to the extent that everyone knows what the acronym represents (e.g., NASA), this is not true of most acronyms. Using an acronym in a communication that is unfamiliar to the recipient interferes with the recipient's understanding of your communication. Even if defined, the use of an unfamiliar acronym slows the reader's ability to absorb the written material. How-ever, while you are warned to avoid acronyms, you should always keep in mind your audience. Readers familiar with commonly used acronyms in, for example, an environmental law practice would expect to see those abbreviations used in com-munications. Indeed, failure to employ such abbreviations might undermine the document. So, as with all communicative considerations, craft the communication to the audience and the purpose.

In conjunction with using familiar terminology, you should also avoid being wordy. This means you should use plain language that the recipients of your com-munication can quickly grasp, rather than attempting to impress your recipients with your vocabulary or sentence length. Writing "the plan was actively effectuated at the time and date when the incorporation of the corporation took place, prioritiz-ing the plan accordingly" not only ineffectively uses the passive voice, but muddles the meaning with pompous language. The writer could just as easily have written, "Because the plan was important, it was activated at incorporation." Professional communication requires that you put effective communication ahead of personal puffery.

Not only should the lawyer avoid being wordy and using pompous language, the practicing attorney should avoid the use of legalese and jargon. Avoid such phrases as "hereby" "hererinafter," "witnesseth," "forthwith," and the like. Gener-ally, your reader must somehow translate this legalese into plain English. This slows the process of receiving the communication. Likewise the use of jargon specific to a particular business or professional community slows the process of absorbing the message.

Just as you avoid fancy language, legalese, and jargon, you should also avoid using clichés. While some clichés may have seemed catchy the first time they were coined, they are often either dull or insulting or they obscure the true meaning of the communication. Therefore, "think of new solutions" is better than "think out-side the box."

D. Once Written, Forever for All the World to See

The most important point to remember about written communications, whether letters, faxes, electronic communications, or telephonic written communications, is that once written and communicated, you have lost control of that communication, and the writing can, and most often will, exist in some format forever. Written communication is a presentation to the world of your ability to communicate effectively, your integrity, your truthfulness, and your commitment to your profession. In short, it can make or break your professional reputation. Once sent, you cannot control who will view your letters, your e-mails, your instant messages, or your text messages. The recipient may willingly transmit them to others, or they may be mistakenly transmitted either by you or the recipient. In any event, what you say and how you say it can be exposed to the world at large. Moreover, the time frame for the potential exposure does not close at any particular point.

> **Cautionary Tale**
> **The Bla, Bla, Bla E-mail**
>
> One would be wise to take a lesson from the tale of Dianna Abdala, a young attorney entering the practice of law. Dianna was slated to begin work for a law firm, but decided to renege via e-mail. What ensued was a lively e-mail exchange between Diana and her potential employer, in which Diana expressed her desire to reap 100% of the benefits that she "sewed" and later chastised her potential employer, for not getting the agreement in writing like "a real lawyer would." Diana's parting e-mail merely said "Bla, bla, bla." The potential employer passed her e-mail onto a friend who, in turn, passed it on throughout cyberspace. Dianna and the "bla, bla, bla" e-mail became notorious.[5]

E. Special Confidentiality Issues Related to E-mail and Faxes

Model Rule of Professional Conduct 1.6 outlines a lawyer's duty to maintain confidentiality with respect to client information related to the lawyer's representation of the client. Comments 16–17 specifically discuss the lawyer's duty to act competently to preserve confidentiality. The comments warn that the duty to maintain confidentiality includes a duty to "act competently to safeguard [client] information . . . against inadvertent or unauthorized disclosure by the lawyer or other persons who are participating in the representation of the client or who are subject to

---

5. Sacha Pfeiffer, *2 E-Mailers Get Testy, and Hundreds Read Every Word*, THE BOSTON GLOBE, Feb. 16, 2006.

the lawyer's supervision."[6] The comments further provide that if a communication contains client information, "the lawyer must take reasonable precautions to prevent the information from coming into the hands of unintended recipients."[7] While the comments make it clear that if the type of communication has a "reasonable expectation of privacy," the lawyer is not required to take special security measures. But he may be required to take special precautions if the method of transmittal does not afford that reasonable expectation of privacy. In determining whether special precautions are warranted, two main factors are to be considered: "the sensitivity of the information and the extent to which the privacy of the communication is protected by law or by a confidentiality agreement."[8]

While electronic and fax communications between two private parties are purportedly private, there are a number of circumstances that make them less so than communication by formal letter. The nature of electronic communication in itself is more public than a private formal letter. The method of transmittal is via a more public "highway," and the opportunities for interception or for the sender to inadvertently send the communication to the wrong recipient are greatly increased. In addition, with respect to e-mail communication, if a private party's work e-mail account is used, that account is likely subject to review by the person's employer, and e-mail communications using that account may be viewed as "owned" by the employer.

Considerations for Written Communications

1. Follow the general considerations for communications.

2. Follow ethical rules and requirements for firm names and letterheads.

3. Pay attention to structure.

4. Seek clarity and avoid ambiguity.

5. Craft your written communication carefully, recognizing that writing is forever.

6. There are special security considerations for fax and e-mail.

Several steps can be taken to ensure the confidentiality of electronic communications and fax communication. If you are representing an individual in his or

---

6. MODEL RULES OF PROF'L CONDUCT R. 1.6 cmt. 16 (2008).

7. *Id.* cmt. 17.

8. *Id.*

her individual capacity, request that a private e-mail or private fax account be the primary transmittal mechanism. Be cautious when you send e-mail that you or your staff has entered the appropriate e-mail address. When you send a fax, be cognizant of entering the correct telephone number. In addition, a confidentiality statement should be appended to the e-mail or fax communication that notifies inadvertent recipients of the communication that the communication is confidential, that an unintended recipient should not read the communication, and that the unintended recipient should notify the sender of the inadvertent transmittal.

III. Letters

Hard-copy communications refer to communications that employ a "hard" method of transmitting the information—that is, not only can the communication be viewed by looking at a hard copy of the document, but there would be no communication without such a hard copy. Thus, while you can generate a hard copy of e-mail and instant messaging, and even telephone messages (transcripts), the means of communicating is not embodied in that document itself, but rather the means of communicating is electronic or verbal. However, when the communication occurs by letter or fax, the hard copy is the communication itself and, as a lawyer, you must keep in mind various ethical and court rules, as well as notions of professionalism, in creating and using hard copy to communicate. Remember, all of the guidelines for written communication in general still apply.

The most frequently used method of hard-copy communication is a letter. Lawyers communicate by letter frequently, and a lawyer's professional reputation can be enhanced or crippled by the way the lawyer communicates in letters. The key to any professional communication is to focus the communication on the recipient. That is, have you focused all aspects of the communication so that it clearly and effectively conveys the information to the recipient? Thus, while the reputation of the lawyer is lawyer-focused, that reputation will be professionally enhanced by being recipient-focused. To create a recipient-focused letter that will in turn enhance your professional and ethical reputation, you must adhere to the requirements for general communications and written communications noted above. In addition, you must plan the letter, format the letter in a professional manner, and consider the appearance of the letter.

A. Planning

A lawyer must spend time planning before writing. The planning process requires determining the purpose of the letter, as well as investigation and inquiry. A formal hard-copy letter should never be sent without first discerning the purpose of the letter. Is it merely to convey documents attached to the letter? Is it a letter of engagement? Is it a demand letter? In determining the purpose of the letter the lawyer should decide whether a hard-copy letter is the best method for communicating the particular information. Once the purpose of the letter is defined, the lawyer must make diligent investigation and inquiry to acquire all of the necessary facts to support the purpose of the letter. For example, if it is a demand letter, the lawyer must research the law and facts. Researching the facts often means conducting an inquiry of what happened. Generally, it is insufficient to merely interview the client to determine the underlying facts for a demand letter. Thus, regardless of the type of hard-copy letter to be sent, you must determine the purpose and conduct appropriate inquiry into the law and facts.

B. Format

A lawyer must adhere to acceptable business format in composing hard-copy letters, regardless of the recipient. If the lawyer does not follow formal business letter conventions, the recipient may not understand the nature of the communication. The essential format components of a business letter include a dateline, the address of the sender, the address of the recipient, a subject line, a greeting or salutation, the body, the closing, the signature, and identification of enclosures.

1. A Dateline

A dateline clarifies for the recipient the timeliness of the communication. The dateline should generally be the date that the letter is *mailed*. In some professional communications, it is appropriate to use the date that the letter is dictated or written; however, because dates are essential to timely filing deadlines related to legal procedures, in the practice of law, business letter dates should reflect the date the letter is mailed.

2. The Address of the Sender

If the letter is written on letterhead, the address of the sender will appear in the letterhead. In such case, the letterhead must conform to the concepts noted above in section II.A. Otherwise, the address of the sender appears following the dateline. The name and address of the sender should clearly convey the profession of the sender.

3. The Address of the Recipient

The address of the recipient should include the name and address of the recipient. If the recipient has a title, the title should be used. If the communication is directed to the recipient in her business capacity, the name of the business entity with whom the recipient is connected should be noted and the communication should be directed to the recipient at that business address. If the communication is directed to a recipient in a personal, rather than business capacity, the personal address of the recipient should be used, unless it is not discoverable.

4. Re or Subject Line

It is customary in legal communication to include a "re" or "subject" line following the address of the recipient. In a professional letter, the re or subject line should be short and direct. If the subject clause is related to a particular case, the case should be identified along with a short description of the contents of the letter. Your subject line should sufficiently identify the subject of the letter, but you should avoid making it too lengthy or complicated.

5. Greeting or Salutation

Every hard-copy letter should contain a formal greeting or salutation. It is generally acceptable to use the salutation "Dear" in business correspondence. The greeting should be followed by addressing the recipient, typically by using the recipient's professional title. In the professional setting, the lawyer should not dispense with "Mr.," "Ms.," and the like. Rarely should you address a recipient by their first name, even when you are otherwise on a first-name basis with the recipient. While Joe Lawyer may socialize with Jane Lawyer, he should address her as "Ms. Lawyer" in professional communications.

6. Body

The body of the letter should pay particular attention to all of the preceding admonitions related to communications in general and written communications in particular. If a response is requested, clearly state that you expect a response and identify the exact time within which you expect a response.

7. Closing and Signature

A professional letter should have a formal closing such as "very truly yours," "truly yours," or a similar closing. Following the closing, a signature block should identify the name of the sender and provide space for a signature.

What Closings Are OK?

- ✓ Sincerely
- ✓ Sincerely yours
- ✓ Very truly yours
- ✓ Truly yours
- ✓ Cordially
- ✓ Cordially yours
- ✓ Respectfully
- ✓ Respectfully yours

---

8. Identification of Enclosures

If enclosed documents have specific names, as is the case with contracts and pleadings, use the specific name of the document to identify the enclosure. Be sure to provide the recipient with some context for the enclosure.

C. Appearance

To a certain extent, the correct formatting noted above will provide a professional appearance to the letter. A few minor details that further promote a professional appearance include creating white space, using appropriate font type and size, and avoiding the use of capitals and italics. While large-scale structure and small-scale structure are created by putting words together into comprehensible sentences, placing sentences into structured paragraphs, and joining paragraphs into a structured writing, the use of white space to identify breaks in the structure will assist the reader in receiving the information. Thus, create sufficient white space within the format and within the body, particularly between paragraphs, to delineate the structure of the letter.

Considerations for Hard-Copy Letters

1. Follow the general considerations for communications.

2. Determine the purpose of your letter.

3. Research the law and facts.

4. Letter format should include:
   - ✓ Dateline
   - ✓ Sender Address
   - ✓ Recipient Address
   - ✓ Subject Line
   - ✓ Greeting
   - ✓ Body
   - ✓ Closing
   - ✓ Signature
   - ✓ Identification of Enclosures

5. Create white space to delineate structure.

6. Use Times or Garamond font no smaller than 11 point.

7. Avoid capitals and italics.

Another consideration for making the communication easier for the reader to comprehend is using the correct font size and type. Generally, serif fonts, such as Times or Garamond, are considered to be the easiest fonts to read. Whatever font you choose, you should generally avoid artistic or frilly fonts. Ideally, font size should be no smaller than 11 point font. However, keep in mind your audience; at times, even 11 point font is too small for the particular recipient.

Using capitals and italics for emphasis is self-defeating. In written form, using all capital letters appears as shouting at your reader—hardly a professional manner of communicating. Italics are difficult to read. If you must choose one, use italics combined with a bold font, but avoid overusing any format for emphasis.

IV. ELECTRONIC COMMUNICATIONS

Electronic communications have posed the biggest problem for lawyers, as well as other business leaders. Because electronic communications have such an informal "feel," and can be sent instantaneously, it is often easy for the lawyer to forget that she should have the same professional concerns, and should craft electronic communication with the same degree of thought and care, as with other forms of communication. Here, the primary concerns include communicating effectively, keeping it "formal," and taking precautions against dissemination.

A. Choosing Electronic Communication

While the concept of choosing an appropriate communication is discussed above, it is particularly important to review that discussion with respect to electronic communications. If a client, colleague, employer, judge, or other recipient is not familiar with or rarely uses electronic communication, then you should avoid using it with them, even for informal communication. Further, most formal communication should be in the form of formal letter unless the recipient has insisted upon electronic notification. Choosing whether to use electronic communication ultimately affects your ability to communicate. Be cautious in selecting this "informal" type of communication. It is appropriate for setting meeting times, for brief updates, or in response to brief, nonsubstantive questions. It is best left for informal communications with recipients who are open to using electronic means of communication.

B. E-mail Considerations

There are a variety of e-mail considerations that affect the lawyer's ability to communicate effectively and professionally. Some of these e-mail considerations are related to format, while others are not.

Subject Line

Every e-mail has a place for a subject line. To communicate effectively, the lawyer should use this subject line. The subject line description should be specific, short, and, if it is urgent, should indicate that it is an urgent matter. Also, if it is appropriate to send a lengthy e-mail, you should include the term "long" in the subject matter clause to alert the recipient that the e-mail is lengthy and will take some time to read.

Order of Recipients

The order of recipients in an e-mail communication may seem insignificant to someone accustomed to informal e-mail communication. However, there generally is a hierarchy of authority in a legal practice, and professionalism requires the attorney to structure communications in a manner that appropriately reflects that hierarchy. If you are aware of a hierarchy within an organization or structure, the recipients should be listed with the recipient having the most authority first. If you are not aware of such a hierarchy or are unable to discern the levels of authority, the recipients should be listed in alphabetical order. It may seem unimportant to you, but it is often important to the recipients where they fall in a recipient list. This is also a consideration when determining whether someone should appear in the "To" category of recipients or the "CC" (carbon or courtesy copy). Recipients in the "To" category are those to whom the content of the e-mail directly applies. People in the "CC" category are copied for informational purposes. Be judicious in choosing to copy individuals in e-mail correspondence. Lawyers are busy and not inclined to be copied on matters not relevant to their practice. It is your responsibility as a professional lawyer to determine who appropriately falls into these categories.

Greeting or Salutation

Do not neglect to use a greeting or salutation in your e-mail. Generally e-mail salutations are less formal; however, if the e-mail is being used as a replacement for a letter, it is best in law practice to use the same greeting or salutation that you would use in the letter. If the e-mail is being used more informally (in place of a memo or phone call), the salutation may simply be the person's name followed by a comma. Generally, even the informal e-mail should have some sort of greeting.

Proper Punctuation and Grammar

Remember that an e-mail communication is still a written communication. You should employ the same rules regarding punctuation, grammar, and capitalization that you employ in any other written communication. Avoid the use of exclamation points or using all capitals for emphasis; both give the appearance of screaming at the recipient. Don't use emoticons or informal abbreviations—known as electronic shorthand—commonly used in informal e-mail, informal text messaging, and informal instant messaging (e.g., "lol" for laugh out loud, or "btw" for by the way).

Closing

As with greetings, you should not neglect a closing merely because the communication is in an electronic format. If the communication is simply a replacement for a formal letter, you should select as formal a closing as you would for a letter, such as "yours truly." Even if you have discerned that the communication is appropriately less formal, do not neglect to at least close with your name. Following your closing, a professional communication should clearly indicate the person sending the communication. It is best to set up a signature that appears as the last part of your e-mail message. It should identify you by first and last name, your address, your phone number, and your e-mail address.

Think Before You Forward

It seems obvious that a professional does not forward jokes, chain e-mail, spam, and the like to his clients, opposing counsel, and judges. In the contemporary workplace, the e-mail inbox is well-used, and very few will appreciate receiving messages that are not work-related. Be respectful of those that you work with by avoiding inundating them with e-mail entertainment. Remember, what is entertaining to you may not be entertaining to your workmates.

C. Instant Messaging and Text Messaging

Instant messaging and text messaging are not widely used in the practice of law. Instant messaging is when an individual communicates directly with another person in real time via computer. Text messaging is communicating with others by short messages that appear on a cellular telephone screen. There is a great opportunity for misunderstanding because of the informal and limited nature of the communication; therefore, these types of communication should be avoided. They should only be used as a replacement for a telephone communication when the individual cannot be contacted by telephone. Be advised that there are a number of rules specifically relating to limitations on attorney solicitation and advertisement that are discussed below in section VI. These rules include limitations on instant messaging and text messaging.

D. Sending an Electronic Communication

The biggest pitfall in sending an electronic communication is making sure that you send the communication to the appropriate party. If you are selecting a group in your address book, be very careful that you wish all of the members of that group to be recipients. Your professionalism and integrity are undermined by sending e-mail to unintended recipients. Further, an attorney must be careful not to reveal client confidences to persons who are not privileged. Thus, when you are representing Defendant A in a lawsuit and the attorneys for Defendants B, C, D, and E comprise a group in your e-mail address book, be careful when you are discussing potential defenses you share with B, but that are detrimental to C, D, and E.

In determining whether you are sending an e-mail to the appropriate party, consider how the recipient will use that e-mail in the future. Perhaps Jane at the Big-Bad Firm is my girlfriend today, but she may not be tomorrow. Will she reveal my inappropriate communications in the future when our relationship has ended? Will she reveal to other friends and colleagues that I disclosed personal information (although perhaps not confidential) about my client? Will those friends and colleagues pass my communication on to my employers?

Cautionary Tale
Look Before You Send![9]

In 2003, Jonas Blank was a summer associate at Skadden Arps. Jonas replied to an e-mail message from his friend saying that "I'm busy doing jack sh---. Went to nice 2hr sushi lunch today . . . . Spent the rest of the day typing e-mails and bullsh—g with people." Unfortunately, Jonas sent his e-mail to all of the lawyers in the firm's underwriting group. Within minutes, Jonas was called on the carpet and required to write an apology to the attorneys who had received the e-mail. Did he survive? Yes . . . barely.

E. Web Sites

The Web site is a useful tool that is often used by a lawyer or law practice to communicate the professional qualifications of the lawyer or lawyers in the practice. Thus, it is generally designed with the intention of creating a professional Web site. Pictures and text on such a Web site should relate only to the law practice, the professional capacity of its lawyers, and general identifying information about those lawyers. Personal photographs and commentary should be avoided. Further, lawyers must be careful to comply with ethical rules regarding communications by a lawyer concerning the lawyer's services. Those rules are discussed at greater length below in Section F.

In addition to specific ethical rules, the ABA Best Practice Guidelines for Legal Information Web Site Providers establish "best practices" for lawyers "who offer

---

9. Ben McGrath, *Oops*, THE NEW YORKER, June 30, 2003 *available at* www.thenewyorker.com/archive/2003/06/60/030630ta_talk_mcgrath.

legal information, documents and other services to the public."[10] While the intro-duction to the guidelines indicates that lawyers who follow the guidelines will be less likely to run afoul of ethical requirements, a lawyer must still consider how the ethical rules of professional responsibility might be implicated. That is, you should not assume that following the guidelines will ensure ethical compliance; however, following the guidelines will assist in achieving that goal. As such, the guidelines are helpful in outlining additional considerations of professionalism, specifically for Web site providers.

Contact Information

The first guideline advises that contact information should be comprehensive. Each page of the site should identify the lawyer, firm, or organization that has cre-ated the Web site. Additionally, the site should provide the name, mailing address, telephone number, and e-mail address of the lawyer or organization.

Materials Should Be Dated

If substantive materials are provided on the Web site, the provider should indi-cate when those materials were created and last updated.

Limits on Jurisdiction Should Be Clear

Any jurisdictional limits on substantive materials should be noted.

Clearly Characterize Nature of the Information

The guidelines state that "[w]hen a site provides only legal information, the provider should give users conspicuous notice that legal information does not con-stitute legal advice."

Provide Helpful Links

A legal Web site should provide helpful links to other sources of information. Annotated information about the link that allows the reader to evaluate the cred-ibility and relevance of the link is also suggested.

Use Legal Citations

If you would use legal citations in other writing you should incorporate those citations on the Web site.

Provide Useful and Appropriate Referrals

Direct your reader to other sources that will assist them in finding legal solu-tions, including directions for obtaining legal advice.

---

10. For more information please see www.abanet.org/elawyering/tool/practices.shtml.

Obtain Permissions

The guidelines advise that "[p]roviders should obtain permission to use content from other providers."

Terms and Conditions

If the site has terms and conditions attached, it should "clearly and conspicuously provide users with information about the provider's terms and conditions of use."

Privacy Statement

Privacy and security policies should be clear and conspicuous.

F. Blogs and Electronic Social Networks

Blogs and electronic social networks are increasingly used by lawyers, but are not typically used as part of the traditional law practice. They are mentioned here to remind lawyers that these electronic communications, while not intended to play a part in a lawyer's professional life, may very well be viewed by others as illustrating the lawyer's professional character. Employers and clients routinely scan Myspace, Xanga, Facebook, and other social networking sites. Google searches often disclose blogs, clubs, and groups that lawyers have created or that they are merely a member of. These electronic postings are considered to be public information having few, if any, privacy implications. To maintain integrity and professionalism in the legal community, you should limit your participation in these electronic activities. When participating, you should proceed with extreme caution, posting only those comments, photographs, opinions, and writings that you would be willing to share with clients, colleagues, employers, judges, and others in the legal community.

Blogging Cybertrails[11]

In 2007, Democratic presidential contender, John Edwards, hired two bloggers to assist with his campaign. While the popularity of the bloggers provided the impetus for their being hired, it was soon discovered that some of the postings on their blogs were in the style of liberal rants, including foul language and blatant anti-Catholic statements. Initially, Edwards stood by his bloggers; ultimately, they were dismissed from the campaign.

---

11. Howard Kurtz, *A Blogger for Edwards Resigns After Complaints*, Washington Post, Feb. 13, 2007, at A04.

V. TELEPHONE COMMUNICATIONS

Telephone communications are essential to any business, including the practice of law. We have all used the telephone and because it is such an integral part of our communications in our personal lives, we do not always deliberately consider how we should appropriately use telephone communications in our professional lives. Your ability to communicate and leave messages will have a considerable impact on those with whom you interact in your law practice. You must plan your communications, be aware of your speaking voice, use appropriate formalities, be respectful of time considerations, leave appropriate messages, and construct appropriate mailbox messages.

Before you make a telephone call, spend a few moments determining the purpose of your call and who the best contact would be to achieve your purpose. For example, a telephone call to the judge assigned to your case to determine the date a document was filed would be inappropriate. In that situation, a call to the clerk of court's office would be more appropriate. Specifically and deliberately identify what you hope to achieve in making a telephone call. If settlement negotiations have begun and you hope to further those negotiations by telephone, have in mind what specific progress you hope to make through the phone call. Outline a plan of action and carry it through to the extent possible.

When you make a telephone call, identify yourself and your connection to your law firm or organization. If you reach a receptionist, be prepared to give a one or two sentence summary of the purpose of your phone call. Make it simple and easy to relay.

Part of having a plan before making a telephone call is having a plan for leaving a voice message for the recipient. Keep voice messages short and succinct. Clearly identify yourself and your contact information. State your purpose in one or two brief sentences. Tell the recipient what action you would like the recipient to take. Is a return telephone call necessary? If there are time constraints, inform your recipient of those constraints.

In telephone communications in your practice, you should employ your "business voice and language." That is, do not slip into sloppy syntax, grammar, and slang because you are using your cellular phone. When you answer the telephone, the best method of answering is to identify yourself and, perhaps, the law firm or organization with whom you are associated. If you use your cellular phone for both personal and business calls, always answer your cellular phone in a professional manner. In such case, you may drop the self-identification, but you should at least answer with a formal "hello." Think carefully about the greeting used on your business and cellular phone. Is it appropriately professional to be heard by clients, opposing counsel, and perhaps judges?

Return phone messages promptly. Do not delay responding to voice messages. It is better to respond that you will provide a more detailed and thorough response at a later time than to fail to respond at all. A good rule of thumb is to return all phone messages within twenty-four hours.

Be honest about your availability. If you are unavailable because you are working on another matter, it is acceptable to instruct support staff to merely indicate that you are unavailable. It is better to honestly indicate your unavailability without providing a lengthier explanation than to instruct your support staff to give the stock answer that "he/she is in court" when it isn't true. Your integrity and honesty lie at the heart of your relationships with clients, judges, cocounsel, opposing counsel, and court personnel.

Your voice mail message should be crafted professionally. Identify yourself and your association with your business. If you will be away for an extended period of time (more than twenty-four hours), you should direct the caller to an alternative contact in the event of a time-sensitive matter. Do not try to be creative or funny in crafting your voice mail message. If you use your cellular phone for both work and personal calls, your voice mail message should conform to business expectations.

VI. CONTACTING POTENTIAL CLIENTS AND ADVERTISING

There are a number of ethical prohibitions that relate to attorney advertising and communication with potential clients. Because these prohibitions apply across the continuum of the various methods of communication—oral, telephonic, written, and electronic—this section address those prohibitions and how they impose limitations on the lawyer's communications.

The primary model rules related to advertising and solicitation appear in Chapter 7 of the Model Rule of Professional Conduct. Rule 7.1 prohibits "false or misleading communication about the lawyer or the lawyer's services." A communication can be false or misleading by commission or omission. Thus, a communication that contains a material misrepresentation of fact or law violates the rule, as does a communication that is materially misleading as a whole because it omits facts. Clearly, then, any statement made by a lawyer about his services, whether that statement be oral, written, or electronic, is governed by this rule.

While false and misleading statements are prohibited, Model Rule of Professional Conduct 7.2 does allow attorney advertising in writing, recorded, or electronic communications within certain parameters. Generally, as noted by comment 5, those parameters prohibit a lawyer from paying "others for channeling professional work." However, the rule allows a lawyer to pay reasonable costs of advertisements. That is, an arms-length transaction in which the lawyer pays the going rate for an advertisement will not constitute a violation of this rule. The rule also allows the lawyer to "pay the usual charges of a legal service plan or a not-for-profit or qualified lawyer referral service." The rule further allows for a lawyer to buy a law practice from another lawyer so long as the lawyers adhere to Model Rule of Professional Conduct 1.17 in the purchase and sale transaction. A lawyer is also permitted to receive referrals in limited circumstances. Of particular importance under this rule is that when an attorney advertises, that communication must "include the name and office address of at least one lawyer or law firm responsible for its content."[12] In sum, advertising is allowed; you may pay for advertising in certain formats; and either you or your firm must stand behind the content of the advertising.

Model Rule of Professional Conduct 7.3 addresses direct contact of potential clients. In general, the rule prohibits a lawyer from direct live contact solicitation of potential clients unless the potential client is a lawyer or has a special prior relationship with the lawyer, such as a family member or a close, personal relationship. Direct live contact solicitation specifically includes "in-person, live telephone, or real-time electronic contact." A lawyer may solicit prospective clients beyond the exception group (other lawyers and those having a special prior relationship with the lawyer) so long as the communication is not "direct live contact" solicitation. However, all solicitation is prohibited if the prospective client has indicated that she does not wish to be solicited or if the solicitation uses coercion, duress, or harassment. Further, written, recorded, or electronic solicitation must "include the words 'Advertising Material' on the outside envelope, if any, and at the beginning and ending of any recorded or electronic communication,"[13] unless the recipient falls within the "lawyer/special relationship" exception noted above. To summarize, in-person, live telephone, or real-time electronic solicitation is almost always prohibited; written, recorded, and electronic communication that is not real time is almost always permitted; and written, recorded, and electronic communication must include the words "Advertising Materials" in specific places on the communication.

One further permission allowed by Model Rule of Professional Conduct 7.3 is that a lawyer "may participate with a prepaid or group legal service plan operated by an organization not owned or directed by the lawyer that uses in-person or telephone contact to solicit memberships or subscriptions for the plan from persons who are not known to need legal services in a particular matter covered by the plan."[14]

Model Rule of Professional Conduct 7.4 addresses the limitations on communicating specific fields of practice and specialization by an attorney. Generally, a lawyer may communicate the fact that he practices in a particular area of law or does not practice in a particular area of law. Designation of "Patent Attorney" requires that the lawyer be admitted to patent practice before the United States Patent and Trademark Office. Designation of "Proctor in Admiralty" may be used by a lawyer engaged in admiralty practice. A lawyer may not represent that she is a specialist certified in

---

12. MODEL RULES OF PROF'L CONDUCT R. 7.2(c) (2008).

13. *Id.* 7.3(c).

14. *Id.* 7.3(d).

a particular area of law unless the lawyer has been certified, the certifying body has been approved by an appropriate state authority or the American Bar Association, and the lawyer identifies the certifying body's name clearly in the communication.

Be mindful that rules 7.1, 7.2, and 7.4 apply to all communications in any form. Model Rule of Professional Conduct 7.3 contains various limitations on solicitation and applies differently to different forms of communication.

The Ten Commandments of Attorney Advertising and Solicitation

1. A lawyer may advertise.

2. A lawyer may not use false or misleading advertising of any kind.

3. Usually a lawyer cannot pay for client referrals, but a lawyer can pay for advertising.

4. A lawyer shall include on each advertisement the name and address of a lawyer or law firm responsible for its content.

5. Most direct live solicitations (including in-person, live telephone, or real-time electronic) are almost always prohibited. Remote solicitations are almost always allowed.

6. If a solicitation communication is allowed, it must include words "Advertising Materials" on it in specific places.

7. A lawyer may not participate in certain prepaid plans that use live solicitation.

8. An attorney may communicate particular fields of law in which he practices.

9. Certain special designations are allowed in very limited circumstances and certification representations are very limited.

10. Firm names and letterheads must comply with rules of advertising and solicitation.

VII. COMMUNICATION WITH CLIENTS WITH DIMINISHED CAPACITY

Model Rule of Professional Conduct 1.14 identifies situations "[w]hen a client's capacity to make adequately considered decisions in connection with a representation is diminished, whether because of minority, mental impairment or for some other reason." Under that rule, the lawyer must continue "as far as reasonably possible, [to] maintain a normal client-lawyer relationship with the client."[15] While the remainder of that rule does not deal with client communications, it is apparent that the lawyer must take into account the client's diminished capacity in considering how to communicate with the client.

Rule 1.14 provides:

> When the lawyer reasonably believes that the client has diminished capacity, is at risk of substantial physical, financial or other harm unless action is taken and cannot adequately act in the client's own interest, the lawyer may take reasonably necessary protective action, including consulting with individuals or entities that have the ability to take action to protect the client and, in appropriate cases, seeking the appointment of a guardian ad litem, conservator or guardian.[16]

When a legal representative has been appointed or exists as a matter of law (a parent of a minor for example), it is usually appropriate for the attorney to communicate fully with that appointed party. However, you should also be aware of those situations in which communications with the legal representative would not be in the best interest of the diminished capacity client. For example, in some situations the parents, while natural guardians and legal representatives of a child, are not the appropriate persons to represent the child's interests in the particular client matter. In such case, the attorney should seek appointment of another legal representative for the child.

Assuming that the attorney has identified the appropriate legal representative and defined the duty to communicate with that representative, the attorney's duty to communicate with the client still continues. Comment 2 to Rule 1.14 recognizes that "[e]ven if the person has a legal representative, the lawyer should as far as possible accord the represented party the status of client, particularly in maintaining communication." In practical terms, this means that where a diminished capacity client has a legal representative, the lawyer must communicate fully with both the legal representative and, to the extent possible, with the diminished capacity client as well. The lawyer should keep in mind that full communication with both a legal representative and a diminished capacity client does not mean identical communication. Therefore,

---

15. *Id.* 1.14(a).
16. *Id.* 1.14(b).

you must tailor the communication to each, which, at times, may require you to transmit the same information in more than one format.

In the situation where a diminished capacity client is neither a minor nor someone whose capacity is so diminished as to require the appointment of a legal representative, then the attorney assumes all of the duties of communication to client outlined in this chapter. However, the communication must be crafted so that the diminished capacity client can understand the substance of the communication and make decisions about such information. Where a diminished capacity client asks family members or other persons to participate in the communication with the lawyer, the lawyer must "keep the client's interests foremost and . . . must look to the client, and not family members to make decisions on the client's behalf."[17] Thus, the diminished capacity client continues to be the decision maker, and communications between attorney and client should reflect that authority.

VIII. ATTORNEY COMMUNICATION WITH ORGANIZATIONAL CLIENTS

The question arises as to whom an attorney should communicate with when the client is an organization. Pursuant to Model Rule of Professional Conduct 1.13, "a lawyer employed or retained by an organization represents the organization acting through its duly authorized constituents." Thus, when the organizational client is a legal entity, communication with the organization, whether it is a client engagement letter or some other communication, it will necessarily be directed to an authorized constituent of that organizational client.[18] An organizational client is defined not only as an incorporated client, but also includes other types of legal entities. In the case of an incorporated client, the appropriate constituents will be the officers, directors, employees, and shareholders. If the organizational client is not an incorporated organization, the lawyer will communicate with other appropriate constituents, including those persons holding "positions equivalent to officers, directors, employees and shareholders."[19] Thus, in directing your communication to the appropriate audience, you must first consider the nature of the organization.

---

17. *Id.* 1.13 cmt. 3.

18. *Id.* cmt. 1.

19. *Id.*

3

COMMUNICATING CONFLICTS OF INTEREST

Chapter 2 identified and discussed a number of general considerations that apply to all communications in the representation of clients. Communications with respect to conflicts of interest are also generally applicable. That is, if a conflict of interest exists, it must be communicated to the client and, in some cases, the representation can continue if informed consent is obtained. Because identifying conflicts of interest and communicating those conflicts appropriately is so essential to ethical and professional communications, this chapter is devoted to it. There are a number of ethical rules that particularly focus on conflicts and communication of conflicts-related issues. In addition, to maintain professionalism and a trustworthy attorney-client relationship, the attorney must deal with conflicts ethically and delicately.

This chapter focuses on identification of conflicts and determining whether conflicts are consentable, in addition to communications related to conflicts. While identification of conflicts and their consentability is not of itself "communication," they are addressed here because appropriate identification of conflicts is necessary to determine when and how the conflicts must be communicated. Thus, Section I of this chapter focuses on identifying conflicts of interest, identifying whether a conflict is consentable, and what communication must occur to continue with a consentable conflict. Section I also identifies particular circumstances that may create a conflict when the attorney and client are involved in business transactions and identifies additional circumstances that may require the client's informed consent. Section II of this chapter changes the focus of conflicts from current clients to former clients, focusing on identifying and communicating with former clients about conflict situations.

I. IDENTIFYING AND COMMUNICATING CONFLICTS WITH EXISTING CLIENTS

A. General Conflict Rules

1. Identifying Concurrent Conflicts

Under Model Rule of Professional Conduct 1.7, an attorney is prohibited from representing a client when "the representation involves a concurrent conflict of interest" unless the conflict is a consentable conflict. If it is such a consentable conflict, the attorney must obtain informed consent.

Under Model Rule of Professional Conduct 1.7, a concurrent conflict of interest occurs when

(1) the representation of one client will be directly adverse to another client; or

(2) there is a significant risk that the representation of one or more clients will be materially limited by the lawyer's responsibilities to another client, a former client or a third person or by a personal interest of the lawyer.[1]

The first question is how the lawyer identifies "directly adverse" interests. Identification of concurrent "directly adverse" interests in the litigation setting is more straightforward than identifying them in the transactional setting. In the litigation setting, the lawsuit identifies the adverse interests of the parties. In the context of the lawsuit, there will be winners and losers, and thus opposing interests are easy to discern. If a lawyer represents party A against party B in a lawsuit, her representation of B in another legal matter would clearly present a conflict.

The identification of concurrent conflicts of interest between clients is sometimes more challenging in the transactional setting. The positioning of the clients need not be adverse *in the particular transaction* to be considered to be "directly adverse" under the subsection (1) of the Model Rule. Comment 6 notes as an example that "if a lawyer is asked to represent the seller of a business in negotiations with a buyer represented by the lawyer, *not in the same transaction, but in another, unrelated matter,* the lawyer could not undertake the representation without the informed consent of each client."[2] Thus, if the lawyer is a transactional lawyer, she must be more vigilant in determining what might be considered directly adverse.

Similarly, there is a broad array of concurrent conflicts that do not create a situation of clients being "directly adverse" under subsection one, but nonetheless

---

1. MODEL RULES OF PROF'L CONDUCT R. 1.7(a) (2008).

2. *Id.* 1.7 cmt. 7.

constitute adverse interests under subsection (2) of Model Rule of Professional Conduct 1.7(a). Where there is no direct adverse interest, comment 8 notes that a conflict may still exist where "there is a significant risk that a lawyer's ability to consider, recommend or carry out an appropriate course of action for the client will be materially limited as a result of the lawyer's other responsibilities or interests." These types of conflicts are more likely to arise in transactional lawyering. Thus, the comment continues, a lawyer asked to represent multiple clients in a joint venture is likely to create a conflict because it is likely that such a situation would materially limit "the lawyer's ability to recommend or advocate all possible positions that each might take because of the lawyer's duty of loyalty to the others."[3] Therefore, in many instances, a concurrent conflict will exist where you are asked to represent multiple participants in the same business transaction.

Likewise, representation of multiple participants in estate planning often gives rise to conflicting interests between clients. As indicated by comment 27, conflicts are likely to arise when an attorney is asked to draft wills for clients who are family members. Similarly, conflicts may occur when the attorney is asked to draft estate planning documents for one family member and other family members participate in the process.

Even more complicated are the instances in which conflicts may exist between clients who are not involved in the same legal transaction. In those instances, the attorney must consider a variety of factors to determine whether the representation will materially limit the lawyer's ability to represent either client, including, "the duration and intimacy of the lawyer's relationship with the client or clients involved, the functions being performed by the lawyer, the likelihood that disagreements will arise and the likely prejudice to the client from the conflict."[4]

It is important to note that you must also be aware of conflicts of interest not only among clients, but also between a client and a third party, or between you and your client. The most likely conflicts between lawyer and client are identified in Model Rule of Professional Conduct 1.8 and include situations in which the lawyer will acquire some pecuniary interest as a result of the relationship. You should be aware that the rule may not outline all types of conflicts and that such conflicts may arise in other transactional lawyering settings not specifically identified in the rule.

2. Identifying Whether the Concurrent Conflict is Consentable

If a concurrent conflict defined under Model Rule of Professional Conduct 1.7 exists, the rule allows the lawyer to represent the client if

---

3. *Id.* cmt. 8.
4. *Id.* cmt. 26.

(1) the lawyer reasonably believes that the lawyer will be able to provide competent and diligent representation to each affected client;

(2) the representation is not prohibited by law;

(3) the representation does not involve the assertion of a claim by one client against another client represented by the lawyer in the same litigation or other proceeding before a tribunal; and

(4) each affected client gives informed consent, confirmed in writing.[5]

While the rule appears to allow the lawyer to represent conflicting interests in some situations by providing informed consent, subsections (b)(1)–(3) indicate that there are certain circumstances in which a lawyer will not be able to represent clients with conflicting interests, regardless of the possibility of informed consent. Whether a client may consent to the conflict depends on the circumstances of the situation. It is doubtful that a conflict is consentable when the clients' interests are "fundamentally antagonistic" to each other.[6] However, if there is not that degree of adversity, the representation is not prohibited by law, and the clients do not have claims against one another in litigation, dual representation may be allowed by obtaining informed consent.

According to comment 18 to Rule 1.7, "[i]nformed consent requires that each affected client be aware of the relevant circumstances and of the material and reasonably foreseeable ways that the conflict could have adverse effects on the interests of that client." Importantly, if a lawyer is required to obtain informed consent due to a concurrent conflict in interest, then, generally each lawyer associated with that lawyer in a firm is imputed to have the identical concurrent conflict of interest and is required to obtain informed consent.[7]

3. Obtaining Informed Consent

Obtaining informed consent is the process of communicating the risk of conflicting representation to the client and obtaining the client's agreement to the continuing representation. Rule 1.0(e) of the Model Rules of Professional Conduct specifically defines the parameters of an acceptable informed consent as an "agreement by a person to a proposed course of conduct after the lawyer has communicated adequate information and explanation about the material risks of and reasonably available alternatives to the proposed course of conduct." As noted by comment 6 to Rule 1.0, the communication identifying the subject of the informed consent should include (1) "a disclosure of the facts and circumstances giving rise to the situation," (2) "any explanation reasonably necessary to inform the client or

---

5. *Id.* 1.7(b).

6. *Id.* 1.7 cmt. 28.

7. *Id.* 1.10.

other person of the material advantages and disadvantages of the proposed course of conduct," and (3) "a discussion of the client's or other person's options and alternatives." In sum, you have an obligation to outline the facts giving rise to the conflict, to advise the client of the advantages and disadvantages of the lawyer's representation, and to advise the client of other options that the client may have.

As noted by Model Rule of Professional Conduct 1.7(b)(4), where consentable conflicts exist, the informed consent must be in writing. Model Rule of Professional Conduct 1.0 defines "writing" as "a tangible or electronic record of a communication or representation, including handwriting, typewriting, printing, photostating, photography, audio or videorecording and e-mail. A 'signed' writing includes an electronic sound, symbol or process attached to or logically associated with a writing and executed or adopted by a person with the intent to sign the writing."[8]

Comment 20 to Rule 1.7 expands on the notion of what is required with respect to obtaining consent from the client confirmed in writing. That comment states that "[s]uch a writing may consist of a document executed by the client or one that the lawyer promptly records and transmits to the client following an oral consent."[9] Further, while it is preferable to give the client a copy of the document simultaneously with the client providing the consent, it is acceptable if the client receives the document within a reasonable time after the consent. Interestingly, comment 20 also emphasizes the need to communicate orally with the client about the substance of the consent and indicates that the written document is not intended as a substitute for an oral discussion, but to "impress upon clients the seriousness of the decision the client is being asked to make and to avoid disputes or ambiguities that might later occur in the absence of a writing."[10]

**Advising of Concurrent Conflicts and
Obtaining Informed Consent**

1. You must advise both orally and in writing:

   - The facts and circumstances giving rise to the conflict.

   - The pros and cons of continued representation in spite of the conflict.

   - Other options available to the client.

2. In addition, it is wise to have the client sign an agreement to continued representation.

---

8. *Id.* 1.0(n).
9. *Id.* 1.7 cmt. 20.
10. *Id.*

In summary, where a conflict exists, the lawyer must, in both an oral conversation with the client and in writing, identify the facts giving rise to the conflict, advise the client of the advantages and disadvantages of the lawyer's representation, and advise the client of the other options that the client may have. Further, it is wise to obtain the client's written execution of his or her consent to the representation.

B. Lawyer's Participation in Business Transactions

While some ethics rules concern general conflicts, Model Rule of Professional Conduct 1.8 identifies rules that are specifically applicable to transactional client conflicts. This section addresses particular transactional situations in which a lawyer has a conflict of interest with the client as well as the communication that must occur in order for the attorney to continue representation of the client.

Model Rule of Professional Conduct 1.8(a) provides:

> (a) A lawyer shall not enter into a business transaction with a client or knowingly acquire an ownership, possessory, security, or other pecuniary interest adverse to a client unless:
>
> > (1) the transaction and terms on which the lawyer acquires the interest are fair and reasonable to the client and are fully disclosed and transmitted in writing in a manner that can be reasonably understood by the client;
> >
> > (2) the client is advised in writing of the desirability of seeking and is given a reasonable opportunity to seek the advice of independent legal counsel on the transaction; and
> >
> > (3) the client gives informed consent, in a writing signed by the client, to the essential terms of the transaction and the lawyer's role in the transaction, including whether the lawyer is representing the client in the transaction.[11]

Thus an attorney has a conflicting interest when engaged in any business transaction with the client or has a pecuniary interest that is adverse to the client. As noted by comment 1, this provision is intended to prevent "the possibility of overreaching when the lawyer participates in a business, property or financial transaction with a client."[12] It is important to keep in mind that the requirements of subsection (a) apply even if the transaction that is at issue is unrelated to the attorney's representation of the client. The comment is clear that the rule specifically applies to (1) a lawyer's sale of goods or services related to the practice of law, such as the sale of title insurance or investment services; and (2) a lawyer's purchase of property from estates that she represents.[13]

---

11. MODEL RULES OF PROF'L CONDUCT R. 1.8(a) (2008).

12. *Id.* 1.8 cmt. 1.

13. *Id.*

As is clear from subsection (a), business transactions with a client are not strictly prohibited; rather, a lawyer must follow a protocol of communication to avoid overreaching in such situations. The first requirement of subsection (a) is that the transaction at issue must be fair and reasonable to the client. In addition, the "essential terms [of the transaction must] be communicated to the client, in writing, in a manner that can be reasonably understood."[14] Further the client must be informed in writing "of the desirability of seeking the advice of independent legal counsel" and must be given the opportunity to obtain such advice. Finally, not only must the attorney obtain the informed consent of the client, in writing and signed by the client, to both the essential terms of the transaction, as well as the lawyer's role in the

---

What Must a Lawyer Do Before Entering into an Allowable Business Transaction with a Client

A. The lawyer should communicate in a written document to the client the following:

- An explanation of the essential terms of the deal in a way that the client can understand them.

- An explanation of the material risks of the proposed transaction.

- An explanation of the material risks of the lawyer's involvement.

- The existence of reasonable alternatives.

- An explanation of why it would be a good idea for the client to obtain independent counsel.

B. The client's informed consent must be in writing, signed by the client, and must indicate the following:

- The client's consent to the essential terms of the deal.

- The role the lawyer will play in the deal.

C. The lawyer must determine if there is a concurrent conflict governed by Rule 1.7, and, if so, he must follow the communication requirements of that rule as well.

---

14. *Id.* 1.8 cmt. 2.

---

transaction, but also, "when necessary, the lawyer should discuss both the material risks of the proposed transaction, including any risk presented by the lawyer's involvement, and the existence of reasonably available alternatives and should explain why the advice of independent legal counsel is desirable."[15]

Comment 3 to Rule 1.8 notes that when the client anticipates that the lawyer will be representing the client in the transaction or "when the lawyer's financial interest poses a significant risk that the lawyer's representation of the client will be materially limited by the lawyer's financial interest in the transaction," the attorney must comply not only with the protocol required by Model Rule of Professional Conduct 1.8(a), but also with the requirements of communication and disclosure compelled under Model Rule of Professional Conduct 1.7. That is, you must first determine whether the concurrent conflict is such that you may not represent the client at all. If you may represent the client under Model Rule of Professional Conduct 1.7, "the lawyer must disclose the risks associated with the lawyer's dual role as both legal adviser and participant in the transaction . . . [m]oreover, the lawyer must obtain the client's informed consent."[16]

C. Other Situations Where the Lawyer Must Obtain Informed Consent from an Existing Client

In addition to the situations identified in sections above, there are a few additional situations in which a potential conflict may arise. In these instances, the attorney must communicate the conflict to the client and obtain informed consent. First, an attorney may not "use information relating to the representation of a client to the disadvantage of the client unless the client gives informed consent."[17] This is similar to the precautions that must be taken when an attorney wants to enter a business transaction with the client. For example, a lawyer may obtain information about a client's business tactics in the course of representation and pass that information on to a competitor of the client who, in turn, uses that information to obtain a competitive advantage over the client. This use of information is only allowed if the client has given informed consent to the disadvantageous use of the information. That is, according to the definition of informed consent, the client must agree to the use of the information after the lawyer outlines the facts, advises the client of the advantages and disadvantages, and advises the client of other options that the client may have. The client then must provide consent, preferably in writing, to the use of such information and/or continued representation by the lawyer.

Another situation in which an attorney must obtain informed consent is when a party that is not a client wishes to pay for the lawyer's services. Model Rule of Professional Conduct 1.8(f) provides:

---

15. *Id.*

16. *Id.* cmt. 3.

17. *Id.* 1.8(b).

A lawyer shall not accept compensation for representing a client from one other than the client unless:

(1) the client gives informed consent;

(2) there is no interference with the lawyer's independence of professional judgment or with the client-lawyer relationship; and

(3) information relating to representation of a client is protected as required by Rule 1.6.[18]

As noted by comment 11, there are many situations in which a lawyer is asked to represent a client where a third party has agreed to pay for the lawyer's services. For example, a friend, an employer, or a family member may agree to pay for the services. However, the interests of third parties who are compensating the attorney may differ greatly from the interests of the client. Such interests include "minimizing the amount spent on the representation and in learning how the representation is progressing."[19] When the circumstances otherwise allow a lawyer to accept compensation from a third party for the representation of the client, the lawyer must obtain informed consent. Generally, the lawyer must advise the client that the third party is paying the cost of representation and must identify that third party. If a concurrent, but consentable, conflict of interest exists under Rule 1.7(a), the consent must be confirmed in writing. Even where not required, it is preferable to obtain written confirmation of the informed consent.

A final situation in which the attorney must obtain the informed consent of the client is when the attorney wishes to disclose information related to the attorney's representation of the client.[20] There may be limited situations where it is advantageous to disclose some confidential information in the course of settlement of a claim. If that is the case, the attorney must be sure to explain the situation fully to the client and obtain the client's informed consent.

II. DUTY TO COMMUNICATE WITH FORMER CLIENTS

In addition to communicating with a client about potential concurrent conflicts the lawyer may have, the Model Rules also require communication with the former clients when the interests of a current client conflict with the interests of the former client. As with other conflicts, before an attorney can determine the extent to which she must communicate a conflict and obtain informed consent, she must first identify whether a conflict exists.

---

18. *Id.* 1.8(f).

19. *Id.* 1.8 cmt. 11.

20. *Id.* 1.6.

Rule 1.9(a) of the Model Rules of Professional Conduct provides:

(a) A lawyer who has formerly represented a client in a matter shall not thereafter represent another person in the same or a substantially related matter in which that person's interests are materially adverse to the interests of the former client unless the former client gives informed consent, confirmed in writing.

While the duty that is addressed here is a duty to communicate with a former client after the representation has ended, it most likely arises at the initiation of the representation of a new client. Thus, you will find that when you begin a new representation, you may be required to communicate with a particular former client in order to accept the representation now before you. If the former client is now represented by counsel, you may not communicate directly with the former client, but must communicate with the former client's attorney.

The first issue, then, is how to identify whether a conflict exists. Such a conflict exists when (1) the matter is the "same or a substantially related matter" of a former client, and (2) the interests of the potential client are "materially adverse" to the interests of the former client. Identifying whether a matter is the "same or substantially related" is often difficult. However, if the matter involves the same transaction in which the attorney actively represented a party, it would constitute the "same" transaction. Thus, as noted by comment 1 to Rule 1.9, "a lawyer could not properly seek to rescind on behalf of a new client a contract drafted on behalf of the former client." A matter is "substantially related" if it encompasses "the same transaction or legal dispute or if there otherwise is a substantial risk that confidential factual information as would normally have been obtained in the prior representation would materially advance the client's position in the subsequent matter."[21]

Therefore, if the lawyer identifies a conflict between a potential client and a former client, the lawyer must proceed with obtaining informed consent from the former client. While the rule and comments do not specifically state what information the lawyer must provide to the former client, the general rule of thumb is to identify the facts giving rise to the conflict. In this situation, it is likely that you should identify the underlying legal matter as well as the identity of the potential client. Additionally, you must clearly explain to the former client that you may be proceeding adversely to their interest. Further, the "former client must have adequate information about the implications (if not readily apparent) of the adverse representation, the fact that the lawyer possesses the former client's confidential information, the measures that the former lawyer might undertake to protect against unwarranted disclosures, and the right of the former client to refuse consent."[22] Because informed consent normally requires an attorney to advise the client of her options, in this situation the attorney must advise the former client that the attorney will not proceed

---

21. MODEL RULES OF PROF'L CONDUCT R. 1.9 cmt. 3 (2008).
22. RESTATEMENT (THIRD) OF THE LAW GOVERNING LAWYERS § 122 cmt. c(i) (2000).

with representation of the potential client without the consent of the former client. The rule requires the attorney to confirm the consent of the former client in writing. While the rule does not require the attorney to obtain the former client's signature on the written confirmation, it clearly would be the best course of action.

Model Rule of Professional Conduct 1.9 identifies an additional situation in which the lawyer must communicate with a former client to obtain his consent to representation of a potential client:

> (a) A lawyer shall not knowingly represent a person in the same or substantially related matter in which a firm with which the lawyer formerly was associated had previously represented a client
>
> (1) whose interests are materially adverse to that person; and
>
> (2) about whom the lawyer had acquired information protected by Rules 1.6 and 1.9(c) that is material to the matter; unless the former client gives informed consent, confirmed in writing.[23]

Essentially, this provision requires you, as a professional attorney, to communicate with and obtain consent from a former client of a firm with whom you were associated, when (1) the former client's legal matter is the "same or substantially related" to the legal matter of a potential client; (2) the former client's interests are "materially adverse" to the potential client's interests; and (3) the lawyer has actual knowledge of information about the former client's legal matter as defined under Rules 1.6 and Rule 1.9(c).

If you are required to obtain consent under this rule, you should identify and communicate to the client the underlying transaction, the identity of the potential client, and the advantages and disadvantages to the former client of your representation of the potential client. Because informed consent normally requires an attorney to advise the client of her options, in this situation you must advise the former client that you will not proceed with representation of the potential client without the consent of the former client. The rule requires the attorney to confirm the consent of the former client in writing. While the rule does not require you to obtain the former client's signature on the written confirmation, it clearly would be the best course of action.

---

23. MODEL RULES OF PROF'L CONDUCT R. 19(a) (2008).

Required Communication with Former Client

1. If a conflict exists between a potential client and a former client under Rule 1.9, the attorney must obtain informed consent of the former client.

   - This usually occurs when representation of a new client is being initiated.

2. If the former client is represented by counsel, the attorney must communicate with the former client's current counsel.

3. Informed consent requires that the attorney communicate in writing with the former client or her counsel:

   - The attorney must identify the former client's legal transaction or matter giving rise to the conflict.

   - The attorney must identify the potential client.

   - The attorney must communicate that she will be acting adversely to the former client's interests.

   - The attorney must inform the former client that she possesses the client's confidential information and identify what the lawyer will do to protect that information.

   - The attorney must inform the former client that he may refuse to consent.

4. The best course is to obtain the former client's signature on the written confirmation of the informed consent.

III. SPECIAL CONSIDERATIONS PERTAINING TO REPRESENTATION OF AN ORGANIZATION: COMMUNICATION WITH CONSTITUENT NONCLIENTS

Another issue that the lawyer must be aware of at the outset of representation, which is more likely in a transactional representation, arises when the attorney is representing an organization, such as a corporation or partnership. As with all conflicts, the essential tasks are identifying the conflict and providing appropriate communication related to the conflict.

As indicated by comment 10 to Model Rule of Professional Conduct 1.13, "[t]here are times when [an] organization's interest may be or become adverse to those of one or more of its constituents." That is, the interests of directors, officers, employees, members, shareholders, and other constituents may not be aligned with the interests of the organization. In this respect, Model Rule of Professional Conduct 1.13(f) provides that when the lawyer represents an organization and the interests of the organization are adverse to the interests of its constituents, the lawyer must advise the constituents that there is a conflict between the organization and the constituent, that the lawyer represents the organization and cannot represent the constituent, that the constituent may wish to seek independent legal counsel, and the communications between the constituent and the lawyer may not be privileged. Although not required by the rule, it would be advisable to provide this information in writing to the constituents. Be sure to observe the general considerations discussed in Chapter 2 concerning written communications.

4

PRETRIAL ADVOCACY

The period of pretrial advocacy is typically considered to be from the time the lawyer is hired to represent a client in a potential lawsuit until the lawsuit actually goes to trial. There are several components of the pretrial advocacy stage that implicate ethical and professional communication issues. The communication that occurs during pretrial advocacy can be broken down into several components:

1. *The engagement.* This initial period involves communication between the attorney and the client about the attorney's competence and the attorney's initial assessment of whether the client has a supportable claim. In addition, the business relationship is memorialized, usually by way of a formal written contract or engagement letter.

2. *The informal investigation.* The "investigation" is that time before a lawsuit is filed when the lawyer is investigating the facts of the case and the law applicable to the case. In this informal investigation period, the lawyer communicates with the client, as well as witnesses and other people who may have knowledge of the case or its subject. The lawyer may also communicate with cocounsel representing other potential litigants and with opposing counsel.

3. *Communications with client.* During pretrial advocacy there is continuing communication with clients. The advice letter is typically prepared when the lawyer has conducted an inquiry into the facts and law sufficient to advise the client whether to go forward with a lawsuit. Additionally, the attorney must address issues that require the informed consent of the client. Furthermore, the attorney has ongoing duties to consult with and provide explanations to the client and to keep the client informed. Finally, the attorney must communicate about lawyer limitations and must be aware of special communication considerations in dealing with diminished capacity clients.

4. *The demand letter.* This is a letter directed to potential opposing parties or their counsel seeking resolution of a legal issue. There are a variety of ethical and professional considerations related to this particular communication.

5. *Honest communications with the court.* As the representation moves to the courthouse upon the filing of the lawsuit, there are specific ethical rules court rules applicable to the lawyer's honest communications with the court.

6. *The initial pleadings.* The lawsuit begins with the filing of the initial pleadings—the complaint and an answer. Much of the legal communication following the commencement of the lawsuit is "on the record" and subject to specific rules of court as well as ethical and professional considerations.

7. *The discovery conference and communication of disclosures.* Once the lawsuit begins, the formal investigation period of "discovery" begins. Court rules impose obligations on the attorneys to communicate by way of a discovery conference. In addition, pursuant to court rules, the attorneys are obligated to make certain disclosures to opposing counsel even in the absence of a specific request.

8. *Discovery.* The communication during discovery is governed by court rules delineating the method and format of the discovery process. There are a variety of discovery methods, including interrogatories, requests for admission, requests for production, and depositions. In addition, there are specific ethical and professional considerations to keep in mind.

9. *Pretrial motions.* A pretrial motion is a method by which attorneys communicate both with other attorneys and with the court. A pretrial motion is the attorney's request for an order from the court. Again, specific rules of court govern this method of communication both as to format and content.

While this chapter deals first with the engagement letter, proceeds to the informal investigation, and then to the advice letter, the timing and order of these stages is not precise. You may do a cursory amount of research and factual investigation, enter into a formal engagement, and follow up with more extensive informal investigation and an advice letter. On the other hand, there may be times when the actual engagement is not entered into until the attorney issues her advice on whether to go forward with the litigation. Additionally, an attorney may send her client advice letters on a variety of issues over the course of the representation and lawsuit. Likewise, informal investigation is an ongoing activity. You are therefore encouraged to keep the time continuum noted above flexible.

The pretrial advocacy stage also includes the initiation of the lawsuit by filing a formal complaint or petition in the appropriate court. In this respect, the lawyer begins communicating not only with court personnel, but with the court (judge) itself. While the informal investigation continues to a certain extent once the lawsuit is filed, the formal investigation via the discovery process begins and is governed by formal rules of discovery. The pretrial advocacy stage includes the filing of additional pleadings and pretrial motions. The sequence of the filing of additional pleadings and pretrial motions and the continuation of discovery is therefore fluid.

As the attorney communicates with a variety of participants during this pretrial advocacy stage, the communications take many different forms—hard copy, electronic, verbal, and nonverbal. The focus, however, is on hard-copy communications. This is particularly true once the lawsuit is filed and the communications occur "on the record." Nevertheless, in all of these formats the attorney is expected to adhere to rules—rules of ethics, court rules (such as the rules of civil procedure), and the like. The attorney should also seek to adhere to the standards of professionalism that will mark her as a respected member of the bar.

I. THE ENGAGEMENT

A. The Engagement Communicates Competence and a Supportable Claim

Before the attorney accepts a representation, she must consider what she is communicating in the act of accepting. First, the attorney's acceptance indicates that she is competent to represent the client. Under Model Rule or Professional Conduct 1.1, lawyers have a duty of providing competent representation to their clients. This means that a lawyer has the "legal knowledge, skill, thoroughness and preparation reasonably necessary for the representation." Thus, in accepting representation, the attorney communicates competence in the matter, whether that competence has been achieved through experience, self-education, or association with another attorney.

In addition, the acceptance of representation communicates that the lawyer has conducted a sufficient inquiry into the facts and law and has concluded from that inquiry that the client has a supportable claim. Both the Model Rules of Professional Conduct and court rules prohibit an attorney from proceeding with frivolous claims. Clearly, the degree of inquiry required of the attorney will vary from one stage in the litigation process to another; nevertheless, the acceptance of the representation communicates that the attorney has conducted an appropriate inquiry and, to the extent of that inquiry, the client's claim is legally and factually supportable.

B. Client Engagement Letters

1. Engagement Letters Should Outline Fees and the Nature of the Agreement, and Should Be in Writing.

Once the attorney determines that the circumstances will allow her to represent a client, she may enter into an attorney-client relationship. In addition to the general considerations noted in Chapter 2 with respect to written communications and letters, there are certain considerations specific to client engagement letters. A client engagement letter is a letter written to the client that sets out the parameters of the attorney-client relationship. While not always required by the ethical rules, you should always define the attorney-client relationship in a formal letter.

Fee arrangements are often addressed in the initial engagement letter and are subject to a number of the ethical rules. Model Rule of Professional Conduct 1.5 prohibits unreasonable fees and provides a number of considerations to determine the reasonableness of the attorney's fees. While an evaluation of the reasonableness of attorneys' fees in particular matters is beyond the scope of this text, the additional provisions in the Model Rules that deal with communication with respect to attorney fees are addressed here. Model Rule of Professional Conduct 1.5(b) provides:

> The scope of the representation and the basis or rate of the fee and expenses for which the client will be responsible shall be communicated to the client, preferably in writing, before or within a reasonable time after commencing the representation, except when the lawyer will charge a regularly represented client on the same basis or rate. Any change in the basis or rate of the fee or expenses shall also be communicated to the client.

While a written statement about fees and the nature of the relationship is not required by the rules, comment 2 notes that "[a] written statement concerning the terms of the engagement reduces the possibility of misunderstanding."[1] Thus, while not required, you are advised to provide a written letter regarding the nature of the relationship and fees.

The engagement letter should also include a description of what types of fees will be charged and how those will be computed. For example, if the fees will be charged at an hourly rate for services, the attorney should indicate for whom such fees will be charged, the specific rate charged by each person who performs on behalf of the client, and the types of services that are included (e.g., preparation, research, travel, interoffice memos, correspondence, etc.). Further, if fees are charged on an hourly basis, the increments in which the hour is divided should be made known to the client. The letter should specifically identify other costs and expenses that the client will be responsible for—for example, long distance telephone charges, messenger or delivery fees, postage expenses, in-office photocopying and its rate, parking, mileage, investigation expenses, and expenses of consultants employed on behalf of the client. All of these specifics help establish the terms of the representation and, therefore, reinforce conventions of professionalism.

The engagement letter should indicate when the client should expect statements from the firm and when payment of outstanding fees and expenses is expected. If you receive a retainer, the mechanism that will be used to draw client funds from the retainer should be carefully outlined. The engagement letter should provide a place where the client signs the letter and acknowledges and agrees to the contents of the engagement letter.

---

1. MODEL RULES OF PROF'L CONDUCT R. 1.5 cmt. 2 (2008).

Finally, if the representation involves a contingent fee, that fee must be in writing. Model Rule of Professional Conduct 1.5(c) provides that "[a] contingent fee agreement shall be in a writing signed by the client and shall state the method by which the fee is to be determined." In stating the method by which the fee is to be determined, the lawyer must specifically indicate the percentage or percentages that the lawyer will receive if the case is settled, if the case goes to trial, and if the case is appealed. In addition, in stating the method of determining the fee, the lawyer must indicate whether "litigation and other expenses [are] to be deducted from recovery; and whether such expenses are to be deducted before or after the contingent fee is calculated."[2] The agreement must also "clearly notify the client of any expenses for which the client will be liable whether or not the client is the prevailing party."[3] Thus, when a contingency fee agreement is the agreed upon method of payment, that agreement must be in writing and contain the specific information outlined by the rule.

In addition to fee information, the engagement letter should identify the scope of the representation with specificity. Usually the identification of a client matter in a letter of engagement indicates that the attorney will represent the client in all aspects of that client matter. However, in some instances, the scope of representation may be limited. Model Rule of Professional Conduct 1.2(c) provides that "[a] lawyer may limit the scope of the representation if the limitation is reasonable under the circumstances and the client gives informed consent." There are various reasons for limiting the representation. At times, a client's conduct may give rise to both civil and criminal considerations, and the lawyer may only be able or willing to address one of those areas. A client may want to limit the representation to initial advice and then make a determination whether to extend the representation. As noted by the rule, however, the limitation on representation must be reasonable. Comment 7 to Model Rule of Professional Conduct 1.2 explains that if the lawyer and client attempt to limit representation to a brief telephone consultation, but that limitation would likely be unreasonable to yield competent advice, the limitation would be considered unreasonable. In sum, the scope of representation must be defined, and a limited representation must be specifically identified and outlined.

In addition to these rules, the Statute of Frauds applicable in most states requires any agreement that is not to be completed within one year to be in writing and signed by the party to be charged. Lawyers are thus advised to have all letters of engagement in writing and signed by the client. If a contingent fee agreement is the method of payment, or if the Statute of Frauds is applicable, the engagement letter must be in writing.

---

2. *Id.* 1.5(c).

3. *Id.*

Client Engagement Letters

1. All client engagement letters should

   - Be in writing.

   - Be signed by the client.

   - Identify the scope of representation.

   - Identify limitations on representation and obtain informed consent where necessary.

   - State what the fee will be (flat fee or hourly fee).

   - Identify how the fee will be computed.

   - Identify the services for which a fee will be charged.

   - Identify expenses that will be charged to the client.

   - Notify the client how often the client will be billed.

   - Communicate when the attorney will expect payment for the amounts billed.

   - If a retainer is used, explain the mechanism by which the attorney will use the retainer.

   - Advise of concurrent conflicts if necessary.

2. Contingent fee agreements must

   - Be in writing.

   - Be signed by the client.

   - State the method by which the fee will be calculated.

   - Indicate how much the attorney will receive if the case is settled, goes to trial, or proceeds to appeal.

   - Identify other expenses to deduct from the recovery.

   - Identify whether other expenses are deducted before or after the contingent fee calculation.

   - Identify expenses that the client will be liable for even if the client does not win or satisfactorily settle the suit.

2. Engagement Letters Should Advise of Client Conflicts

There are a number of instances in which conflicts of interest may arise. These are identified in great detail in Chapter 3, and the attorney is advised to refer to that chapter if a question of conflict of interest is presented. Clearly, if a conflict exists, it should be identified in the engagement letter in the manner outlined in Chapter 3.

II. THE INFORMAL INVESTIGATION

In the informal investigation period the attorney examines the facts and law necessary to determine whether the client should go forward with a lawsuit. There are two components to this process: investigation of the law and investigation of the facts. The former, while essential to the process of determining whether a colorable claim can be made, does not implicate notions of professionalism related to *communication* at the informal investigation stage. The lawyer will ultimately communicate the results of legal research and analysis. This communication arises in the context of advice to clients, provided either orally or in writing, and in persuasive documents like trial and appellate briefs. Those forms of communication are therefore addressed separately in this text. This portion of the text concentrates on an attorney's informal investigation of the *facts*. Investigation of the facts involves obtaining facts by e-mail and letter, as well as interviewing witnesses, and therefore the investigation itself involves communication.

Interviewing witnesses and persons who may have interests adverse to the client in the lawsuit is essential to fact gathering. At this stage, verbal or telephone communications are generally the best and most often used method of interviewing witnesses. However, written communications may also occur in this fact-gathering stage. The attorney may use written communications to obtain documents informally and without resorting to the formal methods of discovery. The attorney may contact potential witnesses by e-mail or formal letter. Thus, you must be mindful of those general considerations related to both oral and written communications outlined in Chapter 2. In addition, during this process, with respect to both written and oral communications, you must be mindful of ethical rules requiring you to be truthful, to limit communication with represented parties, limit communication with unrepresented persons, and limit obtaining information by methods that infringe upon the rights of others

The key ethical consideration related to informal investigation communications is that the lawyer's communication with others be truthful. Model Rule of Professional Conduct 4.1 prohibits a lawyer from making "a false statement of material fact or law to a third person." It also prohibits the lawyer from failing "to disclose a material fact to a third person when disclosure is necessary to avoid assisting a criminal or fraudulent act by a client, unless disclosure is prohibited by Rule 1.6,"[4] which

---

4. *Id.* 1.6.

requires the lawyer to preserve the client's confidences. Thus, when conducting informal investigation communications, the attorney must be truthful and disclose facts necessary to prevent crime or fraud by a client. However, the disclosure is not required if a client confidence would be revealed.

Communication with persons represented by counsel in the matter is prohibited by Model Rule of Professional Conduct 4.2 unless the attorney has obtained the consent of the other attorney, is authorized to speak with the person by law, or has obtained a court order to speak with that person. Thus, when conducting a factual inquiry, you may not communicate with individuals who are represented by counsel about to the matter at hand. This is true regardless of whether that person's interests directly oppose your client's. Comment 3 also makes clear that communication with a represented individual is prohibited "even though the represented person initiates or consents to the communication."[5] If the person initiates the communication, it is incumbent upon the attorney to immediately end the communication.

Model Rule of Professional Conduct 4.3 applies to communications with un-represented persons. As to all unrepresented persons, "a lawyer shall not state or imply that the lawyer is disinterested." In all cases, to avoid a misunderstanding that she is disinterested, the lawyer should identify her client and the fact of representation.[6]

Rule 4.3 not only prohibits an affirmative statement or implication that the law-yer is disinterested, but also requires that "[w]hen the lawyer knows or reasonably should know that the unrepresented person misunderstands the lawyer's role in the matter, the lawyer shall make reasonable efforts to correct the misunderstanding." That is, you have an affirmative duty to correct the misunderstandings related to your role as an advocate. If the unrepresented person has an interest adverse to the attorney's client, the attorney should explain the adversity.

Model Rule of Professional Conduct 4.3 also contains a specific prohibition that the lawyer not give legal advice to those unrepresented persons if those persons "are or have a reasonable possibility of being in conflict with the interests of the client." Thus, when interviewing unrepresented persons who may have interests adverse to the client, you must be careful to avoid the appearance of rendering legal advice to such persons.

Another rule that implicates a lawyer's communication in the informal investiga-tion stage of pretrial advocacy is related to the lawyer's obligation of fairness to third parties. Model Rule of Professional Conduct 4.4 relates to both oral interviewing and obtaining document information. Model Rule of Professional Conduct 4.4(a) provides that "a lawyer shall not use means that have no substantial purpose other than to embarrass, delay, or burden a third person, or use methods of obtaining evidence that violate the legal rights of such person." Essentially, this rule requires the lawyer to keep in mind and elevate the legal rights of others over obtaining

---

5. *Id.* 4.2 cmt. 3.
6. *Id.* 4.3 cmt. 1.

information on behalf of the client. Note, however, that the rule not only requires the lawyer to honor the legal rights of others, but also to avoid means that are meant only "to embarrass, delay, or burden a third person." In other words, you must refrain from using means of obtaining information as improper tactics.

Model Rule of Professional Conduct 4.4(b) relates specifically to documentary information. It provides that "[a] lawyer who receives a document relating to the representation of the lawyer's client and knows or reasonably should know that the document was inadvertently sent shall promptly notify the sender." This rule is intended to deal with a situation where an attorney mistakenly receives a document from an adverse person or attorney. It imposes a duty on the lawyer to communicate with the sender that the lawyer has received the document. Comment 2 to the rule specifically notes that the word "document" includes electronic methods of communication (including e-mail) "subject to being read or put into readable format."[7]

Informal Investigation

1. Identify yourself as a lawyer.

2. Identify your client.

3. Do not make false statements.

4. Do not affirm misleading statements made by others, and correct misunderstandings.

5. Do not have direct contact with a person who is represented by counsel.

6. Do not affirmatively state or implicate that you are disinterested.

7. Do not give legal advice to those whose interests are potentially adverse to your client.

8. Do not use tactics solely to embarrass, delay, or burden.

9. Do not use tactics that infringe on the legal rights of others.

10. When you receive a document accidentally, tell the person who sent it.

---

7. *Id.* 4.4 cmt. 2.

III. COMMUNICATIONS WITH THE CLIENT

Once the engagement letter has been signed the lawyer's official representation begins. One of the initial communications that typically occurs between attorney and client is the advice letter. The Model Rules of Professional Conduct provide guidance in crafting an ethical and professional advice letter.

A. Initial Advice Letters

A lawyer often sends a client an advice letter when he has sufficiently researched the law and facts to advise the client as to her legal options. Generally a formal written letter is the best method of transmitting this advice. A letter creates a record of the advice and reduces the possibility of misunderstanding between lawyer and client. An e-mail communication may be equally effective if the client has indicated a preference. As with other forms of communication, you are advised to determine how your recipient will best receive information. Younger clients, or those familiar with electronic communication, may prefer such a format. Other clients may have an expectation of more formal correspondence, such as a hard-copy letter. In any event, you must take the precautions identified in Chapter 2 to safeguard the confidences of the client and to avoid mistaken transmittal of the information to others. Also, be sure to take precautions to ensure a record of the transmittal and preservation of the communication. Thus, text messaging, where there is no record of the communication, is not advisable.

Note that an initial advice letter may precede or follow the engagement letter. In addition, while an initial advice letter generally sets forth preliminary options to a client, the lawyer will continue to advise the client and draft advice letters throughout the representation. Most of the considerations applicable to an initial advice letter are equally applicable to advice communications provided later in the representation.

Some ethical considerations applicable to advice letters are broadly related to the lawyer's communications with her client in general. Other considerations are unique to the client letter. Model Rule of Professional Conduct 2.1, which addresses the lawyer's role as advisor, provides:

> In representing a client, a lawyer shall exercise independent professional judgment and render candid advice. In rendering advice, a lawyer may refer not only to the law but to other considerations such as moral, economic, social and political factors, that may be relevant to the client's situation.

Comment 1 to Model Rule of Professional Conduct 2.1 makes clear that the duty of providing the client with straightforward, honest advice should not be tempered by a lawyer's hesitancy to present unfavorable information. While it is often uncomfortable to honestly approach unfavorable or unpleasant facts and options, you are under an ethical obligation to do so.

Not only does the lawyer have a duty of candor, but the foregoing comment makes clear that she also has a duty to advise the client as to considerations beyond the scope of purely legal advice. Thus, while your client may have a straightforward case that is likely to prevail, the cost of pursuing that case may be excessive when compared to the potential recovery. In such an event, you must advise the client of the financial implications of proceeding. The extent to which a lawyer must advise a client as to other considerations may be impacted by the sophistication of the client—a more sophisticated client may understand the limitations of receiving purely legal advice. Indeed, some clients may prefer it. However, the lawyer must evaluate whether giving legal advice alone will fulfill her ethical duty to advise; that evaluation must take into account the nature of the client. The duty to advise clients on nonlegal considerations may also require the lawyer to direct the client to consult with professionals in other fields, who may give nonlegal direction needed in a particular situation.

Generally advice letters are drafted and transmitted at the express or implied request of the client. Comment 5 to Model Rule of Professional Conduct 2.1 indicates generally "a lawyer is not expected to give advice until asked by the client." On the other hand, "when a lawyer knows that a client proposes a course of action that is likely to result in substantial adverse legal consequences to the client, the lawyer's duty under [the Rules] may require that the lawyer offer advice if the client's course of action is related to the representation."[8] Further, because Model Rule of Professional Conduct 1.4 imposes a duty upon the lawyer to keep the client informed about matters related to client representation, there may be instances where the attorney may offer unsolicited advice related to the matter. As noted in comment 5, rendering unsolicited advice may sometimes include the duty to advise as to alternative dispute resolution mechanisms if it appears that the client matter may involve litigation.

The advice letter should include a brief statement of the facts upon which the lawyer based her advice. Thus, the attorney necessarily limits the advice to the facts in the knowledge of the lawyer at the time of the advice letter. The advice letter should also contain a summary of the legal rules that affect the outcome of the matter and how those rules apply to the client's facts. The summary of legal rules need not state citations to authority so long as the lawyer can support the legal assertions with authority if called upon to do so.

The advice letter should advise the client of the potential alternative actions. In this respect, pay particular attention to the division of authority between the lawyer and client as outlined by Model Rule of Professional Conduct 1.2. Generally, subsection (a) of the rule requires that the lawyer must "abide by a client's decisions

---

8. *Id.* 2.1 cmt. 5.

concerning the objectives of the representation." Model Rule of Professional Conduct 1.4(a)(2) requires the lawyer to "reasonably consult with the client about the means by which the client's objectives are to be accomplished." In practical terms, this means that in an advice letter you must outline the alternatives available to the client, both in terms of legal action and otherwise. In addition, in order to enable the client to make an informed decision, the benefits and costs of each alternative action should be outlined. You may advise the client as to the course of action that you recommend, but you should be clear in conveying that the ultimate authority rests with the client.

Client Advice Letters

1. Put your advice in a formal letter.

2. Be honest about the potential success of a lawsuit and the costs.

3. State the background facts.

4. Identify the relevant rules of law (although you generally need not provide citations).

5. Support the law in the client file with citations and analysis.

6. Advise client as to all alternatives except for those that are criminal or fraudulent.

7. Advise client of both legal and nonlegal considerations.

8. Let the client know that ultimate authority to choose the means of accomplishing an objective rests with the client.

9. Be clear that a client response is needed, and indicate the time and format for the response.

10. If the client responds by telephone, send a formal letter confirming the client's response.

Model Rule of Professional Conduct 1.2(d) further provides that

> A lawyer shall not counsel a client to engage, or assist a client, in conduct that the lawyer knows is criminal or fraudulent, but a lawyer may discuss the legal consequence of any proposed course of conduct with a client and may counsel or assist a client to make a good faith effort to determine the validity, scope, meaning or application of the law.

Thus, an advice letter should never present criminal or fraudulent conduct as viable alternatives. However, comment 9 notes that this "does not preclude a lawyer from giving an honest opinion about the actual consequences that appear likely to result from a client's conduct."[9] It therefore appears that a lawyer may advise a client that existing conduct may constitute a crime or fraud and advise as to the repercussions of such conduct. Likewise, it appears that a lawyer may advise that a client is legally prohibited from a particular alternative because it involves criminal or fraudulent conduct. Additionally, comment 13 cautions that "[i]f a lawyer comes to know or reasonably should know that a client expects assistance not permitted by the Rules of Professional Conduct or other law" the lawyer must follow Rule 1.4(a)(5), which requires the lawyer to notify the client that he will not be able to proceed with the requested action or assistance.[10]

Because the purpose of the advice letter is to outline the alternative courses of action for the client, the advice letter should specifically identify whether a response is needed, the method by which the lawyer expects a response, and the time frame within which the response is needed. The inclination of many clients is to respond by telephone or e-mail. If the client responds by telephone, the lawyer should send a letter confirming the course of action chosen by the client to memorialize the decisions that the client has made.

B. Duty to Communicate with Clients: Informed Consent

As noted earlier, a lawyer has a duty to advise clients of conflicts of interest. In addition, there are other circumstances in which the lawyer must obtain the informed consent of the client. These circumstances and the requirements of informed consent are laid out in detail in Chapter 3, and the attorney should refer to that chapter for full explanation of instances in which the attorney must obtain the informed consent of the client. One situation that the attorney should be mindful of at the pretrial stage is when disclosure of confidential client information requires informed consent.[11] There may be limited circumstances at the pretrial stage where the client is willing to consent to disclosure of confidential information;

---

9. *Id.* 1.2 cmt. 9.

10. *Id.* cmt. 13.

11. MODEL RULES OF PROF'L CONDUCT R. 1.6(a) (2008).

for example, during settlement negotiations. In addition, in allowing the client to freely choose whether to initiate or continue the representation, both at the pretrial stage and later, the client must be fully informed of conflicts between the attorney and the client, as well as conflicts between other potential and existing clients and the client.

C. Duty to Communicate with Clients: Other Circumstances

Model Rule of Professional Conduct 1.4 institutes additional communication requirements applicable to an attorney's pretrial communications with clients. That rule requires a lawyer to

* * *

(2) reasonably consult with the client about the means by which the client's objectives are to be accomplished;

(3) keep the client reasonably informed about the status of the matter;

(4) promptly comply with reasonable requests for information; and

(5) consult with the client about any relevant limitations on the lawyer's conduct when the lawyer knows that the client expects assistance not permitted by the Rules of Professional Conduct or other law. [12]

In addition, an attorney must "explain a matter to the extent reasonably necessary to permit the client to make informed decisions regarding the representation."[13] While some of these communications have been discussed in the context of client advice letters, the attorney must communicate beyond the advice letter when the identified circumstances arise.

1. Consultative and Explanatory Communication

The requirement that the lawyer "reasonably consult with the client about the means by which the client's objectives are to be accomplished" has been addressed in the context of the initial advice letter.[14] However, this requirement imposes a continuing obligation on the lawyer to make the client aware of the alternative methods of achieving the client's objectives throughout the litigation. Two considerations should be kept in mind when determining whether you must consult with the client and the method by which the client must be consulted. Comment 3 notes that

---

12. *Id.* 1.4(a).
13. *Id.* 1.4(b).
14. *Id.* 1.4(a)(2).

"feasibility" of communication is important in determining whether communication is required at all. Thus, in some situations, such as "during a trial when an immediate decision must be made," the exigency of the situation will preclude consultative communication.[15] However, in most instances of pretrial consultation, such exigencies will not exist.

Assuming that feasibility will rarely be a barrier to communication at the pretrial stage, the second consideration in determining whether a consultative communication is necessary is the importance of the decision. Thus, whether to send a letter to the opposing party by regular mail or courier, while related to the client's objectives, would not generally be deemed a matter of sufficient importance to require client consultation.

If consultation with the client is required, it is generally recommended that such communications occur by formal letter so that the lawyer has memorialized the required communication. To evidence the consultation and consent of the client, it is best to obtain written authorization from the client or send the client a letter confirming that the consultation occurred, that the client was advised, and that the client chose a particular method of satisfying the client's objectives.

Related to the duty to reasonably consult with the client is the lawyer's duty, identified in Model Rule of Professional Conduct 1.4(b), to "explain a matter to the extent reasonably necessary to permit the client to make informed decisions regarding the representation." This rule addresses the lawyer's obligation to explain matters in a manner that enables the client to genuinely participate in deciding the means used to pursue the client's objectives. Comment 5 indicates that "[t]he client should have sufficient information to participate intelligently in decisions concerning the objectives of the representation and the means by which they are to be pursued, to the extent the client is willing and able to do so."[16] In assessing the sufficiency of information, consider the complexity of the client matter and the complexity of the particular course of action under consideration, as well as the sophistication of the client. Sufficiency of information will necessarily depend on the circumstances and be determined on a case-by-case basis.

2. Informative Communication

Model Rule of Professional Conduct 1.4(a)(3) also requires that the attorney "keep the client reasonably informed about the status of the matter." As noted in comment 4, "[a] lawyer's regular communication with clients will minimize the occasions on which a client will need to request information concerning the representation."[17] As a practical matter, clients do not appreciate their lawyer's failure

---

15. *Id.* 1.4 cmt. 3.
16. *Id.* cmt. 5.
17. *Id.* cmt. 4.

to communicate with them on a regular basis. This is particularly offensive when clients continue to receive bills for services. A lawyer should calendar each file so that the client will receive communication from the lawyer on an ongoing basis. Even when there has been no activity on the file, you should communicate with the client at least as often as the client receives a bill. If there has been no activity, the lawyer should communicate that information and the reason for the inactivity to the client. Any action taken on the case should be communicated at the earliest possible time. Even when the attorney is engaging in legal research, the client should be notified of that activity. While each lawyer has hundreds of files, most clients do not, and each client wants the assurance that his legal matter is receiving the attention that he believes it deserves.

The duty to keep the client informed may be fulfilled either by telephone communications, e-mail communications, or formal letters. If the update is of considerable importance or length, a formal letter is the recommended method of communicating. Less significant matters may be communicated by e-mail and telephone. Remember, however, that if the client has received a series of updates by e-mail or telephone, you should occasionally send a formal letter summarizing the status of the case.

In addition to requiring the lawyer to keep the client informed about the case, Model Rule of Professional Conduct 1.4(a)(4) requires the lawyer to "promptly comply with reasonable requests for information." As noted by Comment 4, while the rule requires a prompt response to a reasonable request, "if a prompt response is not feasible, [the rule requires] that the lawyer, or a member of the lawyer's staff, acknowledge receipt of the request and advise the client when a response may be expected."[18] Reflecting the realities of law practice, this rule is tempered by Comment 7, which acknowledges that in some situations "a lawyer may be justified in delaying transmission of information when the client would be likely to react imprudently to an immediate communication."[19] Further, an attorney may withhold information when required to do so by court order or rule. Nevertheless, withholding of information is not allowed merely because it is convenient or advantageous to the lawyer or some other person.

In addition, Comment 4 directs that "[c]lient telephone calls should be promptly returned or acknowledged."[20] Application of this rule is straightforward. The attorney should promptly respond or acknowledge requests for information and promptly respond to or acknowledge telephone communications. While not specifically addressed by the rule or comments, the attorney should also promptly respond to or acknowledge e-mail communications. A good rule of thumb is to respond to telephone and e-mail communications from clients within twenty-four hours.

---

18. *Id.*
19. *Id.* 1.4 cmt. 7.
20. *Id.* cmt. 4.

Case Closed!

One Kentucky lawyer was suspended after he signed three agreements for the dismissal with prejudice of his client's medical negligence claims against the defendants. The lawyer failed to consult with the client before the dismissals, failed to inform the client of the dismissals, and also failed to advise the client that he was no longer employed by the firm.[21]

---

3. Communications about Lawyer Limitations

Rule 1.4(a)(5) requires the attorney to "consult with the client about any relevant limitation on the lawyer's conduct when the lawyer knows that the client expects assistance not permitted by the Rules of Professional Conduct or other law." As noted above, in providing advice to a client, an attorney may not counsel the client to engage in fraud or other criminal conduct. This rule expands on that notion by requiring the attorney to advise the client that the attorney is unable to provide assistance if the assistance expected by the client is impermissible under the rules. Because of the delicate nature of this consultation, it is suggested that the communication of the attorney's limitations be in writing and specifically outline those rules or laws that prohibit the expected behavior.

Duty to Communicate with Clients

1. You must communicate with your client when informed consent is required.

2. You must consult with the client about how the client's objectives will be achieved.

3. You must sufficiently explain matters so that the client can make informed decisions.

4. You must keep the client updated on the status of the client matter.

5. You must promptly respond to requests for information, telephone calls, and e-mails.

6. When the client appears to want improper or illegal assistance, you must communicate the limitations of your representation.

---

21. Kentucky Bar Ass'n v. Taylor, 4 S.W.3d 138 (Ky. 1999).

4. Communication with Clients with Diminished Capacity

There are a number of ethical and professional considerations when communicating with clients who are of a diminished capacity. The lawyer's client communications duties continue; however, those duties may require communicating with a representative of the client, directly communicating with the client in a manner adjusted to that client, or some combination of both. These ethical and professional considerations are dealt with extensively in Chapter 2, and the attorney should refer to that chapter in the event she has a diminished capacity client.

IV. DEMAND LETTERS

A demand letter is a formal demand that another person or entity take responsibility for a legal injury to your client. The demand letter is directed either at the potential opposing party or, if that party is represented, the potential opposing party's counsel. There are various ethical and professional considerations to keep in mind as you set out to draft a demand letter. General considerations regarding written communications and letters outlined in Chapter 2 should be considered as well. Because the communication is a formal request for settlement of a potentially litigable matter, it should generally be memorialized in a formal written letter. The first consideration is to whom the demand letter should be directed. If the potential opposing party is not represented by counsel, the demand letter should be addressed to the potential opposing party. However, Model Rule of Professional Conduct 4.2 prohibits a lawyer from communicating "with a person the lawyer knows to be represented by another lawyer in the matter, unless the lawyer has the consent of the other lawyer or is authorized to do so by law or court order." Thus, when a party is represented, the demand letter must be addressed to the lawyer representing that party.

In the demand letter, the lawyer must clearly identify herself, reveal that she is a lawyer, and identify the person or entity that she represents. Model Rule of Professional Conduct 4.3 prohibits a lawyer, when dealing with an unrepresented person, from stating or implying that the lawyer is disinterested. When the person to whom the demand is directed is not represented, you must be especially sure that you identify the client you are representing. Professionalism also dictates the contents of the letter. The letter should contain a brief outline of the facts known, the legal basis for the demand, a clear demand for a specific action or monetary settlement, and state the time within which the response must be received and the method of transmitting the response.

Model Rule of Professional Conduct 4.1(b) prohibits a lawyer from "knowingly [making] a false statement of material fact or law to a third person" in the course of the lawyer's representation. In the context of a demand letter, this means that the lawyer has a duty to state the facts as candidly as possible. However, comment 2 to the rule notes

[u]nder generally accepted conventions in negotiation, certain types of statements ordinarily are not taken as statements of material fact. Estimates of price or value placed on the subject of a transaction and a party's intentions as to an acceptable settlement of a claim are ordinarily in this category, and so is the existence of an undisclosed principal except where nondisclosure of the principal would constitute fraud.[22]

The comment further states that "[l]awyers should be mindful of their obligations under applicable law to avoid criminal and tortious misrepresentation."[23] In sum, a lawyer has an obligation to be truthful about clear statements of fact; a lawyer does not have an obligation to be truthful as to negotiable items or positions. As a lawyer, you have a duty to know the difference between the two.

Disciplinary Rule 7-105A of the Model Code of Professional Responsibility contains a blanket prohibition against threatening criminal prosecution of the opposing party in a civil matter. The Model Rules of Professional Conduct deliberately do not contain a similar prohibition. In a formal opinion, the ABA Committee on Ethics and Professional Responsibility reasoned

[T]he Model Rules do not prohibit a lawyer from using the possibility of presenting criminal charges against the opposing party in a civil matter to gain relief for her client, provided that the criminal matter is related to the civil claim, the lawyer has a well-founded belief that both the civil claim and the possible criminal charges are warranted by the law and the facts, and the lawyer does not attempt to exert or suggest improper influence over the criminal process. It follows also that the Model Rules do not prohibit a lawyer from agreeing, or having the lawyer's client agree, in return for satisfaction of the client's civil claim for relief, to refrain from pursuing criminal charges against the opposing party as part of a settlement agreement, so long as such agreement is not itself in violation of law.[24]

Nevertheless, while not strictly prohibited, the ABA opinion, along with case law,[25] suggests that in drafting a demand letter in a civil action an attorney should be cautious in threatening criminal prosecution of a matter. She should do so only where (1) the criminal matter is related to the civil claim, (2) the law and facts

---

22. MODEL RULES OF PROF'L CONDUCT R. 4.1 cmt. 2 (2008).

23. *Id.*

24. ABA Comm. on Ethics and Prof'l Responsibility, Formal Op. 92-363 (1992).

25. *See* Committee on Legal Ethics v. Printz, 416 S.E.2d 720, 722–23 (W. Va. 1992) (discussing reasons for abandoning the prohibition, but acknowledging that there are limits on threatening criminal prosecution); State ex rel. Oklahoma Bar Ass'n v. Worsham, 957 P.2d 549, 552 (noting that while threatening criminal prosecution in a civil matter does not, standing alone, violate ethics rules, certain threats of criminal prosecution could violate several of the Model Rules).

support a well-founded belief that both a civil claim and criminal charges are warranted, and (3) the lawyer does not attempt to exert improper influence over the criminal process.

Demand Letters

1. Always use a formal written letter.

2. If a person is represented, the letter must be sent to the person's attorney.

3. Include your identifying information—your name, that you are an attorney, and the name of your client.

4. Outline the facts.

5. Do not make false statements of fact.

6. Know the difference between statements of fact and negotiation technique and negotiable items.

7. Outline the legal basis for your demand.

8. Be specific as to what you are demanding.

9. Identify the action you will take if your demand is not met.

10. Identify the time within which a response must be received.

11. Identify the format of the response expected.

12. Do not threaten criminal prosecution against another potential party unless

    - the criminal matter is related to the civil claim,

    - the law and facts support a well-founded belief that both a civil claim and criminal charges are warranted, and

    - you do not attempt to exert improper influence over the criminal process.

13. Do not threaten criminal prosecution against opposing counsel.

Similarly, the Model Rules do not specifically prohibit threatening criminal prosecution of opposing counsel, but it is likely that such threats are impliedly prohibited. This implication is discussed in Formal Opinion 94-383,[26] which notes that a lawyer has a duty, under Model Rule 8.3(a), to report another attorney's conduct if it "raises a substantial question as to that attorney's honesty, trustworthiness, or fitness."[27] A threat of criminal prosecution implies that the attorney who is threatening has the option of not reporting such conduct. The attorney does not have that option under Model Rule 8.3(a). In sum, the best approach in writing a demand letter is to omit threats of criminal prosecution of opposing counsel.

The final consideration of writing a demand letter is that the lawyer should always include a cautionary statement that the demand letter is being made for settlement purposes only. Pursuant to Rule 408 of the Federal Rules of Evidence and similar state evidentiary rules, certain offers of compromise are not admissible in evidence "to prove liability for, invalidity of, or amount of a claim that was disputed as to validity or amount." Including the statement "Confidential: For Purposes of Settlement Discussion Only" at the heading of the letter is generally sufficient to bring the demand letter within the protection of Rule 408 and prevent its use to prove your client's admission of liability.

V. Honest Communications with the Court

There are several Rules of Civil Procedure and Model Rules of Professional Conduct that impose obligations of honesty on an attorney's communications with the court. The Federal Rules of Civil Procedure are referenced here because most state rules are similar; however, the attorney is cautioned to check the particular local rules governing the cause of action at hand.

This section of the chapter addresses the Federal Rules of Civil Procedure and the Model Rules of Professional Conduct applicable to pleadings and motions. It is important to note that some rules are applicable only to "submissions" to the court, some rules are applicable only to discovery, and other rules are applicable to both. Rules dealing specifically with discovery are dealt with later in this chapter. This portion of the chapter focuses on rules applicable to both formal, written "submissions" to the court, as well as other types of communication lawyers have with the court.

A. Honest Communication in Court Submissions: Federal Rule of Civil Procedure 11

Federal Rule of Civil Procedure 11 focuses on the attorney's honest communications with the court in the process of submitting documents. As a starting point, it is important to keep in mind that Federal Rule 11 does not apply to "disclosures

---

26. ABA Comm. on Ethics and Prof'l Responsibility, Formal Op. 94-383 (1994).
27. Model Rules of Prof'l Conduct R. 8.3(a) (2008).

and discovery requests, responses, objections and motions under Rules 26 through 37."[28] There are, however, other rules that have a similar requirements regarding honesty during discovery and those are discussed below.

As noted in the following sections addressing pleadings and motions, Federal Rule of Civil Procedure 11 requires the attorney or unrepresented party to sign the documents that are filed in a legal action. However, the more significant portion of that rule provides that the act of filing, submitting, or presenting a document is a communication of certification by the lawyer.

Under Rule 11, you as an attorney make certain representations to the court by presenting a document to the court, regardless of whether that presentation is by "signing, filing, submitting, or later advocating" the document. By the submission or presentation of a document, the attorney certifies that to the best of her

> knowledge, information, and belief, formed after an inquiry reasonable under the circumstances:
>
> (1) it is not being presented for any improper purpose, such as to harass, cause unnecessary delay, or needlessly increase the cost of litigation;
>
> (2) the claims, defenses, and other legal contentions are warranted by existing law or by a nonfrivolous argument for extending, modifying, or reversing existing law or for establishing new law;
>
> (3) the factual contentions have evidentiary support or, if specifically so identified will likely have evidentiary support after a reasonable opportunity for further investigation or discovery; and
>
> (4) the denials of factual contentions are warranted on the evidence or, if specifically so identified, are reasonably based on belief or lack of information.[29]

In essence, the attorney who presents a document to the court communicates to the court her certification that she has made a reasonable inquiry and determined that there is both sufficient evidentiary support for the factual allegations or denials and sufficient law to support the legal claims. Further, the attorney certifies to the court that she is not asserting the document for any improper purpose.

The importance of this certification cannot be overstated, because Rule 11 provides sanctions that may be imposed if the court finds that the certification is false. These sanctions may include the imposition of monetary fines on the attorney and

---

28. FED. R. CIV. P. 11(d).
29. *Id.* 11(b).

---

her client.[30] If monetary sanctions are imposed on the attorney, "[a]bsent exceptional circumstances, a law firm must be held jointly responsible for a violation committed by its partner, associate, or employee."[31] Such monetary sanctions may include payment of penalties, as well as payment to the opposing party of "part or all of the reasonable attorney's fees and other expenses directly resulting from the violation."[32] The rule also allows for the imposition of nonmonetary sanctions, which have been held to include dismissal of the lawsuit. Thus, the certification of compliance required by Rule 11 should always be considered by the attorney when she is submitting or presenting a document to the court, whether that document is a pleading, motion, or some other nondiscovery document.

B. ABA Model Rules: Applicable to All Communications with the Court

Similar to Federal Rule of Civil Procedure 11, the Model Rules of Professional Conduct provide:

> A lawyer shall not bring or defend a proceeding, or assert or controvert an issue therein, unless there is a basis in law and fact for doing so that is not frivolous, which includes a good faith argument for an extension, modification or reversal of existing law.[33]

This model rule mirrors a portion of Rule 11. This particular rule, like Rule 11, requires an attorney to support legal and factual assertions that are communicated during the legal process. Because the language of this model rule is not specifically limited to nondiscovery communications, it could be interpreted to apply to discovery as well. Thus, the rule is significant in two respects. First, it may govern a broader set of communication than Rule 11. Second, it permits ethical discipline of attorneys for the prohibited conduct.

In addition to Rule 11 and Model Rule of Professional Conduct 3.1, Model Rule of Professional Conduct 3.3 addresses candor and is implicated when a lawyer communicates with the court. In the context of pretrial procedures, the lawyer is communicating with the court when she files any pleading, when she submits motions, and when she is involved with the court during the discovery process. The rule provides that "[a] lawyer shall not knowingly . . . make a false statement of fact or law to a tribunal or fail to correct a false statement of material fact or law previously made to the tribunal by the lawyer."[34] This particular limitation is quite clear—the lawyer must not mislead the court by false statement of either fact or law.

---

30. *Id.* 11(c).
31. *Id.* 11(c)(1).
32. *Id.* 11(c)(4).
33. MODEL RULES OF PROF'L CONDUCT R. 3.1 (2008).
34. *Id.* 3.3(a).

Further, the model rule prohibits a lawyer from knowingly "fail[ing] to disclose to the tribunal legal authority in the controlling jurisdiction known to the lawyer to be directly adverse to the position of the client and not disclosed by opposing counsel."[35] This particular prohibition typically applies when a lawyer files a motion with the court. In such instance, the lawyer must reveal any adverse controlling authority, even when her opponent fails to disclose it.

The Model Rule also provides:

> [a] lawyer shall not knowingly . . . offer evidence that the lawyer knows to be false. If a lawyer, the lawyer's client, or a witness called by the lawyer, has offered material evidence and the lawyer comes to know of its falsity, the lawyer shall take reasonable remedial measures, including, if necessary, disclosure to the tribunal. A lawyer may refuse to offer evidence, other than the testimony of a defendant in a criminal matter, that the lawyer reasonably believes is false.[36]

This rule clearly prohibits the introduction of false evidence even if the client wants the lawyer to present such evidence to the court. The comments to the rule give the lawyer some direction in this matter. If the lawyer is aware that some of the testimony of a particular witness will be false, but not all of it, the lawyer can call the witness and avoid asking questions that will yield the false testimony.[37] Clearly, the presentation of false evidence is more delicate in the criminal context than in the civil context, and the criminal lawyer must be educated in the parameters of the obligations to the client and obligations of candor to the court.

The model rule also requires a lawyer to take "reasonable" remedial action if the lawyer knows that a person in an adjudicative proceeding "intends to engage, is engaging or has engaged in criminal or fraudulent conduct related to the proceeding."[38] Such remedial measures include "if necessary, disclosure."

In ex parte proceedings, the model rules require a lawyer to "inform the tribunal of all material facts known to the lawyer that will enable the tribunal to make an informed decision, whether or not the facts are adverse."[39] As noted by the comments to the rule, a lawyer can generally rely on the other side to present adverse evidence and facts.[40] However, in cases where the proceedings are ex parte and opposing counsel is therefore not present, the lawyer has a duty to inform the court of all material facts, even those that are unfavorable to the lawyer's position.

---

35. *Id.* 3.3(a)(2).
36. *Id.* 3.3(a)(3).
37. *Id.* 3.3 cmt. 6.
38. *Id.* 3.3(b).
39. *Id.* 3.3(d).
40. *Id.* 3.3 cmt. 14.

Candor to the Court

1. If a lawyer presents a document to the court, it is a certification that
   - ✓ The lawyer conducted a reasonable inquiry of the law and facts and both are supported.
   - ✓ The document is not frivolous.
   - ✓ The document is not presented for an improper purpose.

2. A lawyer may not mislead the court about the law or the facts.

3. A lawyer must disclose controlling adverse authority, even if her opponent does not.

4. A lawyer must not offer false evidence.

5. A lawyer must disclose a person's criminal or fraudulent conduct to the court.

6. In ex parte proceedings, a lawyer must disclose all material facts to the court.

A Watershed Moment in . . . Watershed Moments

In *Goshgarian v. George*,[41] one neighbor was alleged to have frequently disposed of dirty swimming pool water on the property of the other. The lawyer who represented the pool owner argued that the pool owner could do this because the County of Fresno had an easement on the property for draining and disposing of storm drain water. This argument did not fly with the judge who commented that "[o]nly a mind unburdened by the ephemeral shackles of legal training and gloriously free of the stultifying pompousities of precedent and stare decisis could have formulated the epiphanous principle that what the public may do as an entity, so may individual members of the public do, acting in their individual capacities." Communicating a legally arguable position in the pleadings is essential to your credibility before the court!

---

41. 161 Cal. App. 3d 1214 (Cal. Ct. App. 1984).

VI. INITIAL PLEADINGS: THE COMPLAINT/PETITION AND THE ANSWER

The complaint or petition is the formal statement commencing a legal action.[42] As such, it is a formal communication to the opposing party, to the court and its administrative personnel, and to the public. The answer is the formal response to the complaint or petition. It is also a formal communication to not only the opposing party, but to the court, court personnel, and the public. In essence, the complaint and answer communicate the legal and factual basis for the lawsuit. In addition, the initial pleadings serve to discretely define the legal issues and inform the parties and the court of the scope of the evidence. Finally, the initial pleadings begin the communication of the lawsuit "on the record." With the commencement of the lawsuit, the official record of communications and proceedings in the lawsuit also commence.

It is not surprising that there are a variety of court rules, as well as ethical rules and considerations of professionalism, that apply to the format and content of these types of pleadings. In addition to the complaint and the answer, other pleadings may communicate other claims and responses. Thus, a defendant may file a counterclaim; cross-claims may be filed; third-party complaints may be filed; and answers (or replies) to all of these claims may be filed as well. Generally, these additional filings must satisfy the same rules that govern the complaint and answer. Also, it is important to remember that the rules and considerations dealt with in Section III of this Chapter regarding communications with clients continue to apply throughout the representation, including the initial pleadings stage.

The rules of civil procedure for each jurisdiction govern the format and, in some respects, the content of the complaint and the answer. The Federal Rules of Civil Procedure will be referenced here, but most state rules have similar provisions. The attorney is therefore cautioned to carefully review all of the rules of the applicable jurisdiction. This will include not only the applicable state or federal rules of the jurisdiction, but the local rules as well. This section generally lays out many common considerations of communicating the formal legal action and the answer to that formal legal action; however, it does not provide a comprehensive overview of those rules for each jurisdiction.

A. The Complaint and Answer: Format

Adherence to the following recommendations regarding the required format of a complaint is a manifestation of your professionalism as an attorney. A failure to conform to the expectations of the court with respect to your written communications undermines your credibility as an advocate.

---

42. FED. R. CIV. P. 3.

Caption

Rule 10 of the Federal Rules of Civil Procedure governs the format of all pleadings, including the complaint and answer. In every instance, a pleading must have a caption that identifies the name of the court in which the pleading is filed, the docket number, and the title of the pleading. Additionally, the complaint must state the names of all parties. The answer and subsequent pleadings only need to state the name of the first party for each side of the legal action.[43]

Communication of Jury Demand

When a party is entitled to trial by jury, that party may submit a request for a jury trial to the other party and the court. The request must be in writing and must be transmitted to the other party and filed with the court within ten days after the last pleading.[44] If the party seeking a jury trial fails to demand it as required by Rule 38, then the party waives the right to a jury trial.[45] As a practical matter, the plaintiff generally requests the jury as part of the complaint. If the plaintiff has not requested a jury trial, the defendant generally requests a jury trial as part of the answer. In some jurisdictions, the party is required to note the jury demand in the caption of the pleading, even if it is part of another pleading.[46] Conforming the jury request to local rules is an aspect of professional communication.

Separate Statements in Numbered Paragraphs

Likewise, preparing the complaint in a manner that conforms to local rules is evidence of professional communication. The federal rules require the attorney to communicate the claims and defenses in the complaint and answer in numbered paragraphs. Further, to the extent possible, each paragraph should be limited "to a single set of circumstances."[47] In practice, wherever possible, it is best to limit each paragraph to a single sentence.

Introductory Paragraph, Divisions, and Headings

Some aspects of the large-scale structure of the pleadings are dictated by rule; others arise out of less formal conventions of professionalism and practice. It is understood that a complaint and an answer will begin with an introductory paragraph, such as "Comes now, the Defendant, Mr. Rogers, and for his cause of action, states as follows." While the parties have been identified in the caption, the introductory paragraph indicates which party is filing the particular pleading and what it is.

---

43. *Id.* 10.
44. *Id.* 38(b).
45. *Id.* 38(d).
46. *See, e.g.,* Iowa R.C.P. 1.902(2).
47. FED. R. CIV. P. 10(b).

Additionally, a complaint and its counterpart answer generally have a "Parties, Jurisdiction & Venue" heading for the paragraphs that identify the parties, their locations, and the basis for the court's jurisdiction. This section of the complaint and answer follow the introductory paragraph. Following the identification of parties, jurisdiction, and venue, background facts common to all counts are generally stated in a section identified as the "Statement of Facts." Following the Statement of Facts, the complaint and answer are often divided into sections based upon claims and defenses.

Federal Rule of Civil Procedure 10(b) provides that "[i]f doing so would promote clarity, each claim founded upon a separate transaction or occurrence—and each defense other than a denial—must be stated in a separate count or defense." This essentially means that each cause of action should be delineated in a separate count. Further, each affirmative defense that constitutes more than a mere denial to the complaint should be delineated as a separate defense. As a practical matter, the attorney should number each count and label it with some sort of descriptive heading, such as "Count 1—Negligence." Similarly, a counterclaim should contain separate count headings where applicable. If affirmative defenses are stated in an answer, those affirmative defenses should be identified by separate headings in a manner similar to the various counts.

Concise and Direct Exhibits

Federal Rule of Civil Procedure 8(d)(1) provides that "[e]ach allegation must be simple, concise, and direct" and that "no technical form is required." If the attorney chooses to attach a copy of a written document to the complaint or answer, it becomes a part of that pleading for all purposes.[48] Thus, an affidavit appended to a pleading becomes a part of that pleading. Clearly, then, as a matter of professionalism, it is incumbent on the lawyer to review all attachments.

Alternative and Inconsistent Claims and Defenses

The federal rules of civil procedure do not require the claims and defenses of the parties to be consistent. The complaint may state inconsistent and alternative claims for relief, and the answer may assert inconsistent and alternative defenses.[49] The party is often unable at the initial pleadings stage to elect a particular legal theory, and this rule gives the party leeway in both asserting and defending legal claims. Thus, such inconsistent assertions are not unprofessional.

---

48. *Id.* 10(c).
49. *Id.* 8(d)(3).

Special Filing Communication: Disclosure Statements for Nongovermental Corporations

While not a part of the complaint or answer, a nongovernmental corporation is required to file an additional communication when it first appears in an action. It must file a disclosure statement that "(1) identifies any parent corporation and any publicly held corporation owning 10% or more of its stock; or (2) states that there is no such corporation."[50] Because nongovernmental corporations must file this at the time they make their first appearance, this is usually filed concurrently with the complaint or answer.[51] Two copies of such a statement must be filed, and if the information contained in the statement changes, the nongovernmental corporation must promptly file a supplemental statement noting that change.

Signature

Under Rule 11(a) of the Federal Rules of Civil Procedure, every pleading must be signed by the attorney of record. Specifically, both the complaint and answer must be signed. In addition, the pleadings must identify the signer's address, e-mail address, and telephone number. If a document is presented for filing without the attorney's signature, it will be stricken unless the signature is promptly added after the party or the attorney is notified of the omission. As a practical matter, the attorney's signature on the complaint and the answer communicates the attorney's representation of a party to the action. The significance of the signature is addressed in greater detail later in this chapter in the discussion of truthfulness to the court.

B. The Complaint: Contents

Similarly, the complaint and related pleadings must conform to the rules related to content of the document. A failure to include the relevant material required by rule undermines your client's position and your reputation. In some instances, pleadings that do not contain the required content may be stricken and may show a lack of the competence required by the ethical rules. Thus, the content you communicate in pleadings should conform to local rules.

Jurisdiction

Generally, the complaint must identify, in a "short and plain statement," the basis for the court's jurisdiction over the claim. [52] Thus, if the "amount in controversy" is an element of the court's jurisdiction, then the complaint should allege an amount in controversy. Whatever is essential to the court's jurisdiction must be alleged. Claims asserted after the suit is initiated (e.g., counterclaims, cross-claims,

---

50. *Id.* 7.1(a).

51. *Id.* 7.1(b).

52. *Id.* 8(a)(1).

and the like) must also identify the court's jurisdiction if the court does not already have jurisdiction over the claim.

Notice Pleading: The Claim

With respect to the substance of the claim itself, the federal rules require only "a short and plain statement of the claim showing that the pleader is entitled to relief."[53] Generally, this is understood to allow the plaintiff to forego a detailed rendition of the facts of the claim; however, it is also understood that the ethical and professional counsel for plaintiff must allege sufficient facts as to support a claim for relief.

In spite of the general allowance of notice pleading, in some circumstances, more particularity is required. For example, "[i]n alleging fraud or mistake, the circumstances constituting fraud or mistake [plaintiff] must state with particularity."[54] Federal Rule of Civil Procedure 9 imposes special rules and instruction for pleading conditions of mind, capacity, official documents or acts, judgments, time and place, special damages, and admiralty and maritime claims. The lawyer is well-advised to review this rule and similar state and local rules to assure herself whether or not a particular claim requires greater detail for its proper communication.

Demand for Relief

The complaint must also contain a demand for relief.[55] Thus, the complaint generally concludes with a prayer for relief identifying the type of relief sought by the party filing the claim. Generally, the prayer for relief does not identify a specific monetary amount so as not to limit the claimant's damages. For example, Federal Rule of Civil Procedure 54(c) limits a judgment by default so as not to "differ in kind from, or exceed in amount, what is demanded in the pleadings." The professional lawyer must carefully consider the types of damages that may be available in a particular action. For instance, in some jurisdictions attorneys' fees are only allowable by statute. It would be unprofessional to assert the right to these types of damages without the requisite research.

C. The Answer: Contents

In responding to the complaint, the contents of the answer must "admit or deny the allegations asserted against it by an opposing party."[56] Within the parameters of admitting and denying the allegations of the complaint, the lawyer for the defendant has the flexibility to admit in whole, deny in whole, admit in part and deny in part, or, in some jurisdictions, to deny for lack of information. A general denial

53. *Id.* 8(a)(2).
54. *Id.* 9(b).
55. *Id.* 8(a).
56. *Id.* 8(b)(1)(B).

of the entire complaint is permitted only if the "party . . . intends in good faith to deny all the allegations of a pleading—including the jurisdictional grounds . . . ."[57] General denials are not the norm because it is the rare occasion that the defendant can completely deny every allegation of the complaint.

As a matter of presenting a document consistent with the conventions of professionalism, the answer should be a mirror image of the complaint, at least until the point where the answer introduces affirmative defenses, counterclaims, and other claims. As such, the answer should respond to each numbered paragraph of the complaint with a corresponding numbered paragraph in the answer. The rule requires that the denials "fairly respond to the substance of the allegation."[58] Additionally, unless a general denial is appropriate, the "party . . . must either specifically deny designated allegations or generally deny all except those specifically admitted."[59] As a practical matter, these requirements dictate that the responsive paragraphs be written in complete sentences.

The significance of the admissions and denials is that this is the formal communication, on the record, of the defendant's response to the plaintiff's allegations. In most instances, the failure to deny an allegation will have the effect of constituting an admission. Federal Rule of Civil Procedure 8(b)(6) provides:

> An allegation—other than one relating to the amount of damages —is admitted if a responsive pleading is required and the allegation is not denied. If a responsive pleading is not required, an allegation is considered denied or avoided.

Because a complaint requires a responsive pleading—an answer—all allegations except those pertaining to the amount of damages will be considered admitted if not specifically denied. Thus, in order to be an effective advocate, the attorney must be sure to respond to the allegations specifically.

The answer must "state in short and plain terms its defenses to each claim asserted . . . ."[60] The lawyer must be fully aware of the various defenses allowable under Federal Rule of Civil Procedure 12(b)(2)–(5): lack of personal jurisdiction, improper venue, insufficient process, and insufficient service of process. These defenses must either be raised in the answer or in a motion filed *prior to* the answer. If they are not raised in this manner, they are waived.

Further, after the answer has responded to all of the allegations of the complaint, it must assert affirmative defenses.[61] Generally, an affirmative defense is one that would allow the defendant to prevail even if all of the allegations of the complaint

---

57. *Id.* 8(b)(3).
58. FED. R. CIV. P. 8(b)(2).
59. *Id.* 8(b)(3).
60. *Id.* 8(b)(1)(A).
61. *Id.* 8(c).

are true. The rule provides a list of some affirmative defenses, but the attorney must be sure to raise all potential affirmative defenses, even if not appearing on the list, to ensure that she has not waived any.

A General Checklist for Initial Pleadings

1. Every pleading should have a caption.

2. A demand for a jury trial must be timely communicated.

3. Allegations and defenses in the pleadings should be stated in numbered paragraphs.

4. Most pleadings begin with an introductory paragraph.

5. Most pleadings should employ headings and divisions to delineate various claims and defenses.

6. Pleadings usually may assert alternative and inconsistent claims and defenses.

7. Nongovernmental corporations may be required to file disclosure statements.

8. Pleadings must be signed by the attorney.

D. Mechanics of Communicating the Pleadings

A complaint or answer is not fully communicated to the intended parties unless it is appropriately served on opposing parties and filed with the court. While the details and methods of service and filing are beyond the scope of this text, the attorney must be mindful of the rules pertaining to service and filing and should be aware of the local rules that may govern. For example, in many jurisdictions, electronic filing is either accepted or required by local rule.

VII. Discovery Conference and Communication of Disclosures

Earlier in this chapter, the informal investigation process was discussed. In contrast, the discovery process is the formal investigative process. The discovery process begins with a discovery conference and the communication of disclosures.

A. Mandatory Discovery Conference

In most cases, the attorneys are required to conduct a mandatory discovery conference. The purpose of the conference is to discuss possibilities for settlement, to make arrangement for the prediscovery disclosures required under the rule, to discuss issues about preserving discoverable information, and to develop a discovery plan. The attorneys must submit to the court a written report of the discovery plan.[62] The rules anticipate that the discovery plan will be incorporated in the court's scheduling order, which is governed by Rule 16(b) of the Federal Rules of Civil Procedure.

B. Communication of Disclosures

Rule 26(a) of the Federal Rules of Civil Procedure requires the attorneys to communicate certain disclosures to one another once a legal action has begun. While much of the discovery process discussed below requires the attorneys to request information from one another, this is not the case with respect to these disclosures. The communication of these disclosures is required without a request from opposing counsel. Generally, the disclosures relate to information that the disclosing attorney will use to support its claims or defenses. The attorney must consult the rules to determine deadlines that apply to such disclosures. The rules may also set forth certain details that must be included in those disclosures. Generally, all of the required disclosures must be in written form, signed, and served on the opposing party.[63]

The rule requires the attorneys to communicate the identification of persons who are "likely to have discoverable information . . . that the disclosing party may use to support its claims or defenses . . . ."[64] The identification of such persons includes providing opposing counsel with the name of the person and, if the attorney knows the information, the address and telephone number of the person. In addition, the attorney must communicate the subject of that discoverable information to the other attorney.

The rule requires the attorneys to give opposing counsel copies of "all documents, electronically stored information, and tangible things that the disclosing party has in its possession, custody, or control and may use to support its claims or defenses . . . ."[65] In lieu of a copy of such materials, the attorneys may communicate "a description by category and location" of those materials.[66] The rule also requires

---

62. *Id.* 26(f)(1)–(2).

63. *Id.* 26(a)(4).

64. *Id.* 26(a)(1)(A)(i).

65. *Id.* 26(a)(1)(A)(ii).

66. *Id.*

disclosure of any computation of damages and any insurance agreements that may indicate an insurance company who may be liable for any part of the judgment.[67]

Attorneys must also make certain disclosures related to the use of expert witnesses. The attorney is required to indicate whether the expert witness has been hired to specifically provide expert testimony in the lawsuit, or whether the witness is an employee of the client whose job includes regularly providing expert testimony. In addition, the report must include a complete statement of the expert's opinions and the basis for those opinions. Furthermore, the expert witness report requires considerable detail regarding the data and other information underlying the witness's opinion, as well as exhibits, the witness's qualifications, the witness's history of testifying as an expert, and the fees that will be paid to the expert witness. The report must be prepared and signed by the expert witness.[68]

The attorneys are also required to communicate information about the evidence that the attorneys will employ at trial. A witness list must be provided to opposing counsel. The list must identify the name, address, and telephone number of each witness. The attorneys must tell the other party which witnesses' testimony is expected to be presented by deposition at trial. The attorneys must also communicate to opposing counsel the exhibits that will be employed at trial.[69]

With the exception of expert witness reports prepared under Federal Rule of Civil Procedure 26(a)(2), other disclosure communications (under Federal Rule of Civil Procedure 26(a)(1) and (2)), must be signed by "at least one attorney of record in the attorney's own name."[70] The signature must include the attorney's address, e-mail address, and telephone number. As noted previously, the effect of the signature is a certification by the attorney "that to the best of the [attorney's] knowledge, information, and belief formed after a reasonable inquiry . . . it is complete and correct as of the time it is made . . . ."[71] Thus, the attorney is certifying that she has conducted a reasonable inquiry and has reasonably concluded from that inquiry that the disclosures are "complete and correct as of the time" they are made. If the certification is found to be false, the attorney, as well as the party represented, is subject to sanctions, including the reasonable expenses and attorneys' fees caused by the violation.[72]

---

67. *Id.* 26(a)(1)(A)(iii)–(iv).
68. *Id.* 26(a)(2).
69. FED. R. CIV. P. 26(a)(3).
70. *Id.* 26(g)(1).
71. *Id.* 26(g)(1)(A).
72. FED. R. CIV. P. 26(g)(3).

Prediscovery Disclosures

1. Identify persons likely to have discoverable information about the lawsuit.

2. Provide copies of all documents, electronic files, and tangible items the party may use in the lawsuit.

3. Disclose how damages will be computed.

4. Disclose relevant insurance agreements.

5. Identify expert witnesses and information about their opinions.

6. Provide a witness list to opposing counsel.

7. Sign and certify all disclosure communications.

VIII. DISCOVERY

Discovery is the formal investigation process during which the attorneys communicate with one another, as well as with witnesses and other nonparties, to obtain information and evidence for trial. Each court has formal rules governing the discovery process. In this chapter, the Federal Rules of Civil Procedure will be used as

---

Discovery Disaster
Rock, Paper, Scissors

The discovery rules anticipate that the rules will facilitate communication between attorneys and that the discovery process will be conducted in a courteous and professional manner. In most cases, attorneys can and should come to an agreement about when and where to hold depositions without involving the court. The court shouldn't have to resort to ordering the parties to engage in a "rock, paper, scissors" contest to resolve the deposition location. But that's what happened in a Florida case. Professional discovery communication? Hardly.[73]

---

73. Avista Management, Inc. v. Wausau Underwriters Ins. Co., No. 6:05-cv-1430-Orl-31JGG, 2006 U.S. Dist. LEXIS 38526 (M.D. Fla. June 6, 2006).

a reference. However, you must be aware that state and local rules may vary. The federal rules provide general guidelines as to what to expect during the discovery process. In addition, the Model Rules of Professional Conduct are applicable during this stage of the pretrial process. These methods include interrogatories, requests for admissions, requests for production, and depositions.

A. Ethical Considerations of Communication during Discovery

1. Attorney Communication with Nonclients

a) Communication with Witnesses and Unrepresented Parties during Discovery

An attorney's communication with witnesses and unrepresented parties during the discovery process is subject to the Model Rules of Professional Conduct. Model Rule of Professional Conduct 4.1(a) prohibits a lawyer from making "a false statement of material fact or law to a third person." Rule 4.1(b) requires the lawyer "to disclose a material fact to a third person when disclosure is necessary to avoid assisting a criminal or fraudulent act by a client" (unless disclosure is prohibited by Model Rule of Professional Conduct 1.6, which requires the lawyer to preserve the client's confidences). Essentially, Rule 4.1(b) requires that the attorney be truthful when communicating with potential witnesses, other nonparties, and unrepresented parties during the discovery process.

The rule does not, however, allow the attorney to disclose client confidences. Thus, when contacting potential witnesses, nonparties, and unrepresented parties, the attorney should pay particular attention to preserving the client's confidences. Even if the witness is a favorable witness or the unrepresented party is an "ally," the attorney must be mindful that the discussions with these persons are not protected.

When dealing with a person who is not represented by counsel, the attorney should not "state or imply that the lawyer is disinterested."[74] Thus, when dealing with unrepresented persons, the lawyer should identify herself and the client that she represents. If the unrepresented person has an interest opposing the client's, the attorney should explain that to the unrepresented person.[75]

Model Rule of Professional Conduct 4.3 also contains a specific prohibition that the lawyer not give legal advice to unrepresented persons if those persons "are or have a reasonable possibility of being in conflict with the interests of the client." This prohibition has continued viability during the discovery phase. Thus, when communicating with unrepresented persons—whether they be witnesses, other nonparties, or unrepresented parties—who may have interests adverse to the client,

---

74. MODEL RULES OF PROF'L CONDUCT R. 4.3 (2008).
75. *Id.* cmt. 1.

---

the lawyer must be careful to avoid the appearance of rendering legal advice to such persons.

b) Attorney Communication with Parties Represented by Counsel

As previously noted in the discussion of the informal investigation, communication with persons represented by counsel is prohibited by Model Rule of Professional Conduct 4.2 unless the attorney has obtained the consent of the other attorney, is authorized to speak with the person by law, or has obtained a court order to speak with that person. Thus, disclosure and discovery documents should be served upon opposing counsel rather than the opposing party. When conducting a factual inquiry in preparation of discovery documents or for depositions, the attorney may not communicate with individuals represented by counsel, even if they are not in direct opposition to the client's interests. An attorney is therefore prohibited from directly communicating with or obtaining information from coparties. This is true even if the communication appears to be consensual or is initiated by the represented party.[76]

c) Attorney Communication Discouraging Sharing Information

Lawyers may not "request a person other than a client to refrain from voluntarily giving relevant information to another party," except in very limited circumstances.[77] Those limited circumstances exist when

(1) the person is a relative, an employee, or another agent of a client; and

(2) the lawyer reasonably believes that the person's interests will not be adversely affected by refraining from giving such information.[78]

Thus, as a general rule, during both informal investigation and discovery, an attorney cannot discourage potential witnesses or other persons from sharing information with other parties.

2. General Ethical Limitations on Discovery Communications

Model Rule of Professional Conduct 4.4(a) provides that "a lawyer shall not use means that have no substantial purpose other than to embarrass, delay, or burden a third person, or use methods of obtaining evidence that violate the legal rights of such person." Thus, during the discovery process, it is not enough to merely be cognizant of the legal rights of others; the rule specifically requires the attorney to painstakingly avoid embarrassing other persons or causing a delay to or burden on

---

76. *Id.* 4.2 cmt. 3.
77. *Id.* 3.4(f).
78. *Id.*

another person. In short, the lawyer must refrain from using means of obtaining information as an improper tactic.

3. Attorney Communications with Opposing Counsel and Parties

Model Rule of Professional Conduct 3.4(d) specifically applies to communication with opposing counsel and parties during discovery and the pretrial process. It provides that "[a] lawyer shall not . . . in pretrial procedure, make a frivolous discovery request or fail to make reasonably diligent effort to comply with a legally proper discovery request by an opposing party." This rule is straightforward. Discovery communications must be reasonable and nonfrivolous. The attorney must diligently respond to proper discovery requests. In sum, formal discovery communications, like all communications between counsel, must evoke a sense of fairness to the opposing party and opposing counsel.

In addition, an attorney may not "unlawfully obstruct another party's access to evidence."[79] Any communication intended to so obstruct such access is specifically prohibited. This rule applies to both communications with a client or other person directing the person to obstruct such access, and misrepresentative or misleading statements to opposing counsel that would lead to such an obstruction.

B. Discovery: Generally

Most attorneys are familiar with the methods of discovery that embody the communication of relevant information about the case between attorneys, between attorneys and opposing parties, and between attorneys and witnesses. The attorneys may send and respond to interrogatories as well as requests for production; they may request or respond to a request for permission to enter upon land or other property; they may request or respond to a request for physical and mental examinations; they may request or respond to requests for admissions; and they may conduct depositions of witnesses and parties.[80] The methods may be used in any sequence or order.[81] The rules of discovery allow the parties to "obtain discovery regarding any nonprivileged matter that is relevant to any party's claim or defense . . . ."[82] This includes material that will be inadmissible at trial so long as it is "reasonably calculated to lead to the discovery of admissible evidence."[83] In general, the timeliness of communicating discovery and responses to discovery are governed by both the discovery rules and the discovery plan formulated at the discovery conference.

---

79. *Id.* 3.4(a).

80. FED R. Civ. P. Art. V.

81. *Id.* 26(d).

82. *Id.* 26(b)(1).

83. *Id.*

The duty to respond to discovery also requires the attorney to supplement or correct her responses to the extent necessary to complete or correct material information.[84]

There are, however, some limitations on a party's duty to respond to discovery requests. An attorney can deny the discovery of electronically stored information if the attorney determines that the sources of the information are "not reasonably accessible because of undue burden or cost."[85] An attorney's obligation to produce certain materials may be obviated or limited by a protective order of the court. Any party may obtain such a protective order "to protect a party or person from annoyance, embarrassment, oppression, or undue burden or expense . . . ."[86]

Note also that privileged matters are not subject to discovery.[87] Likewise, as a general rule, trial preparation materials are not discoverable.[88] An attorney must affirmatively and specifically express a claim that material is privileged or represents trial preparation materials if the attorney withholds such information.[89] Such an explicit expression of the claim must include a description of "the nature of the documents, communications, or tangible things not produced or disclosed . . . in a manner that . . . will enable other parties to assess the claim."[90] In the process of describing those matters, the attorney must be sure not to disclose privileged or protected information. Thus, to the extent that you claim materials are privileged or protected, you must explicitly assert that claim and provide opposing counsel with sufficient information about the nondisclosed materials to assess the validity of your claim.

The rule recognizes that in some instances, privileged or protected materials are disclosed before such a claim is made. In that event, certain procedures must be followed to ensure the integrity of a claim of privilege or protection. The party making the claim must notify other parties who have received such materials that a claim of privilege or protection is being asserted. Once such a claim is received by a party, that party must take steps to destroy, isolate, or return such materials, and the party is prohibited from using or disclosing the materials to others. Additionally, if the party who has received the material has disseminated it, that party must take steps to retrieve the material. Further, the party who has received the material can produce it, under seal, to the court for a determination of whether the material is legitimately privileged or protected. The information or materials must be preserved during the time that the court is making its determination.[91] Thus, if you receive materials and subsequently a party makes a claim of privilege or protection, you must take steps

---

84. *Id.* 26(e)(1).
85. *Id.* 26(b)(2)(B).
86. *Id.* 26(c)(1).
87. *Id.* 26(b)(1).
88. *Id.* 26(b)(3).
89. *Id.* 26(b)(5).
90. *Id.* 26(b)(5)(A)(ii).
91. FED. R. CIV. P. 26(b)(5)(B).

to protect the privileged or protected nature of the materials until the court makes a final determination.

General Rules Governing Discovery Communications

1. Discovery communication methods may be used in any order.

2. Timeliness of discovery communications is governed by the rules of civil procedure and the discovery plan adopted by the lawyers at the discovery conference.

3. Information may be discoverable even if it will not be admissible at trial.

4. An attorney is under an ongoing duty to supplement responses to discovery in order to correct and complete those responses.

5. An attorney can refuse discovery of electronically stored information if production would be unduly costly or burdensome.

6. A protective court order can limit or negate a duty to produce discovery.

7. Privileged materials and trial preparation materials are generally not discoverable, but an attorney must affirmatively assert the protection of these materials and describe them in that assertion.

8. If privileged materials and trial preparation materials have been disclosed to a party before the other party identifies them as protected, the party who has those materials must take particular steps to ensure the integrity of the protected materials.

C. Effect of Attorney Signature on Discovery Documents

Under the federal rules, an attorney is required to sign discovery documents and that signature on discovery documents is essentially a certification of the attorney's good intentions. Under Federal Rule of Civil Procedure 26(g)(1), discovery documents, including requests, responses, and objections, must be signed "by at least one attorney of record in the attorney's own name." The signature of the

---

attorney on the discovery documents must include the attorney's address, e-mail address, and telephone number. The signature constitutes a certification by the attorney that to the best of the person's knowledge, information, and belief formed after reasonable inquiry

* * *

(B) with respect to a discovery request, response, or objection, it is:

    (i) consistent with these rules and warranted by existing law or by a nonfrivolous argument for extending, modifying, or reversing existing law, or for establishing new law;

    (ii) not interposed for any improper purpose, such as to harass, cause unnecessary delay, or needlessly increase the cost of litigation; and

    (iii) neither unreasonable nor unduly burdensome or expensive, considering the needs of the case, prior discovery in the case, the amount in controversy, and the importance of the issues at stake in the action.[92]

Thus, the signature is essentially a certification both to the court and to the opposing party that the attorney has conducted a reasonable inquiry and that both the law and facts are supported; that the attorney is not serving the discovery request or response for an improper purpose; and that the response or request is not unreasonable nor unduly burdensome or expensive in light of what is at stake in the action.[93] The significance of this certification is that sanctions may be imposed upon both the attorney and the represented party if the certification violates the rule and is "without substantial justification." The reasonable expenses caused by the violation, including attorney's fees, may be imposed upon the violator.[94]

If the attorney fails to sign the discovery document, the opposing party has no duty to act on it. Additionally, the "court must strike it unless a signature is promptly supplied after the omission is called to the attorney's . . . attention."[95]

D. Interrogatories

Interrogatories are written questions served upon another party that the other party must respond to unless that party has a legitimate objection. Thus, the interrogatories and answers are how a party, through her attorney, communicates her need for information and the opposing party, through her attorney, communicates

---

92. *Id.* 26(g)(1)(B).
93. *Id.*
94. *Id.* 26(g)(3).
95. *Id.* 26(g)(2).

the information requested. The scope of interrogatories is generally as broad as the scope of discovery in general; that is, the information requested need not be admissible, but must be "reasonably calculated to lead to the discovery of admissible evidence."[96] Inquiries into facts, opinion, and even legal application are generally permissible.[97] As noted earlier, the time constraints of these communications are limited by rule and the discovery plan of the parties. The number of interrogatories that may be served is also limited by rule, and subparts to questions are included in the computation of how many interrogatories are served. Your obligation as an ethical and professional attorney is to know the detailed requirements of such formal, communicative documents.

When interrogatories are served, the party may answer the interrogatory or the attorney for the party may object to the interrogatory. Each interrogatory must be separately answered. A party's answers must be signed by the party himself under oath.[98] Objections to interrogatories must be signed by the attorney representing the party. Such objections must be specific and if an objection is not made in response to the interrogatory, it is generally waived.[99] If the information requested by an interrogatory can be obtained by reviewing the business records of a party, and either party is equally able to extract the information from those records, a party may respond to the interrogatory by producing such business records.[100]

In sum, you may request information by serving interrogatories on the other party. When you receive interrogatories, you must ask your client to answer those interrogatories unless you have a legitimate objection to any of them. You must provide timely answers or objections to the interrogatories, properly signed by the appropriate party (under oath) or attorney.

E. Requests for Admissions

Requests for admissions are a communication asking another party to "admit, for purposes of the pending action only, the truth of any matters" within the broad scope of discovery.[101] Requests for admissions can be sought for facts, opinions, or the application of law to the facts of the case, as well as to the "genuineness of any described documents."[102] Each request for admission must be a separate statement, and if the request is directed at the genuineness of a document, the document must be attached or made available.[103] If a party fails to timely respond to a request for

---

96. *Id.* 26(b)(1).

97. *Id.* 33(a)(2).

98. *Id.* 33(b).

99. *Id.*

100. *Id.* 33(d).

101. *Id.* 36(a)(1).

102. FED. R. CIV. P. 36(a)(1)(B).

103. *Id.* 36(a)(2).

admission, the matter is deemed admitted,[104] which means that it "is conclusively established."[105] However, it is established only as to the case in which the admission was sought.[106] The court may allow withdrawal of an admission under limited circumstances.[107] Clearly, the wise attorney does not gamble on the possibility that the court will allow an admission to be withdrawn. A timely response to requests for admissions is essential to your client's case.

There are several responses to a request for admission. It may be entirely admitted or denied; it may be admitted in part and denied in part; it may be denied for lack of information; or the party may respond by objecting to the admission. If the substance of a request for admission is not fully deniable, the answer should specifically admit those portions that are truthful and specifically deny those that are not. Similarly, if the answer to a request is a denial, such denial must be specific or detail the specific reason why the party cannot legitimately admit or deny the request. Generally, lack of knowledge can only be asserted as the basis for denial if the party has made a "reasonable inquiry" and the information that she obtained from the inquiry or that is readily obtainable is not sufficient to allow the party to either admit or deny the truth of the matter.[108] If the party objects to a request, the basis for that objection must be specifically identified.[109]

In sum, requests for admissions are not simply a communication that occurs in the process or preparing for trial, but are a unique tool in the attorney's arsenal of trial tactics. A request for admission can constitute a final and conclusive communication by the opposing party as to the truth of an essential matter or issue for trial.

F. Requests for Physical and Mental Examinations

In a lawsuit in which a party's "mental or physical condition . . . is in controversy," the party may communicate a request for a physical or mental examination as a part of the discovery process.[110] This communication is different than other discovery requests because it is a communication to the court; that is, the party is asking the court to order the other party to submit to an examination. A party may also seek a court order requiring "a party to produce for examination a person who is in its custody or under its legal control."[111] Thus, the order may require a guardian to cause the ward to submit to such an examination.

---

104. *Id.* 36(a)(3).
105. *Id.* 36(b).
106. *Id.*
107. *Id.*
108. *Id.* 36(a)(4).
109. *Id.* 36(a)(5).
110. *Id.* 35(a)(1).
111. *Id.*

Clearly, in most lawsuits, examinations are out of the ordinary. And the order for an examination is more intimate than other discovery requests. Therefore, there are specific requirements in seeking such an order—the party must file a motion, but the motion will be granted only if notice is given to all the parties and the person to be examined and good cause is shown for the medical examination. If an order is granted, it must be particularly limited.[112]

Once an examination is granted, certain obligations of communicating examination reports are imposed upon the party who has requested the examination, as well as upon the opposing party. Essentially, the rules require the party who obtained the examination to deliver, upon request, copies of the examination report to the person examined as well as to opposing parties.[113] In turn, the party against whom the order was entered must deliver copies of reports of earlier and later examinations.[114]

G. Requests for Production

During the discovery process, a party may request documents related to the subject matter of the lawsuit. Again, such documents need not be admissible in evidence, but need only be "reasonably calculated to lead to the discovery of admissible evidence."[115] While the rules related to production generally refer to documents, the rule also allows a party to request electronically stored information and other tangible items. The rule also permits a party to request entry upon land or other property to inspect the land or items related or upon the land.[116]

In order to properly make a request, the request must particularly describe the subject of production or inspection. It must also "specify a reasonable time, place, and manner for the inspection and for performing the related acts."[117] Finally, with respect to electronically stored information, the request must specify the form or forms in which it is to be produced.[118]

The responses to each request must either assent to the request or object to it. Objections must be specific. If the responding party merely wishes to object to the format requested, for example, electronically stored information, such an objection is acceptable, but the party must identify the form in which she wishes to produce the information.[119] In addition, with respect to both documents and electronically stored information, "[a] party must produce documents as they are kept in the usual course of business or must organize and label them to correspond to the categories

---

112. *Id.* 35(a)(2).
113. FED. R. CIV. P. 35(b)(1).
114. *Id.* 35(b)(3).
115. *Id.* 26(b)(1).
116. *Id.* 34(a).
117. *Id.* 34(b)(1)(B).
118. *Id.* 34(b)(1)(C).
119. *Id.* 34(b)(2)(D).

in the request."[120] Additionally, if no specific form is requested, the form in which the electronically stored information is generally kept should be supplied, but only one form is required.[121]

In summary, either party may communicate requests for production, but such requests must be timely and provide specific information. Responses must provide the information in the requested format or in the format in which it is generally stored.

H. Inadvertent Receipt of Documents

Model Rule of Professional Conduct 4.4(b) provides that "[a] lawyer who receives a document relating to the representation of the lawyer's client and knows or reasonably should know that the document was inadvertently sent shall promptly notify the sender." Therefore, when in the course of discovery, the attorney mistakenly receives a document from an adverse person or attorney, it imposes a duty on the lawyer to communicate with the sender that the lawyer has received the document. Comment 2 to the rule specifically notes that the word "document" includes electronic methods of communication (including e-mail) "subject to being read or put into readable form."[122]

I. Depositions

Depositions are a discovery method in which an attorney for a party can ask questions of another party or witness to gain information for trial. Depositions most often involve taking the sworn oral testimony of the party deposed and having that testimony recorded by a court reporter. However, depositions may also be recorded by audio or audiovisual means.[123] Depositions may also be taken by written questions requiring written responses.[124]

The Rules of Civil Procedure govern, among other things, the procedure for taking depositions by written questions, the persons before whom an oral deposition may be taken, the duties of the officer before whom the deposition is taken, the duration of the deposition, whether court permission is required to take the deposition, and how deposition testimony may be used at trial. Many of these procedures and rules are beyond the scope of this text, but the practitioner is cautioned to consult these rules and conform the communicative aspects of depositions to these rules.

---

120. *Id.* 34(b)(2)(E)(i).

121. *Id.* 34(b)(2)(E)(ii–iii).

122. MODEL RULES OF PROF'L CONDUCT 4.4 cmt. 2 (2008).

123. FED. R. CIV. P. 30(b)(3).

124. *Id.* 31.

Of note, however, is that depositions are most often arranged by stipulation of the parties and are most often taken as oral depositions. Every other party to the lawsuit must be given written notice of the time and place of the deposition, as well as the name and address, if known, of the deponent.[125] A witness's presence is ensured by using a subpoena ordering the deponent to attend the deposition.[126]

As provided in Rule 30(c), generally, "[t]he examination and cross-examination of a deponent proceed as they would at trial under the Federal Rules of Evidence." Therefore, all of the considerations of professionalism and ethical rules pertaining to examination and cross-examination of witnesses at trial as discussed in Chapter 5 should be reviewed and followed in the communication with witnesses during deposition.

You should note that objections that might be raised at trial must be similarly communicated on the record at the deposition in order to preserve those objections. The rule dictates that the objections "be stated concisely in a nonargumentative and nonsuggestive manner."[127] In a deposition, the testimony still proceeds following the objection. Only in very limited circumstances, such as when it is "necessary to preserve a privilege" and other limited circumstances, may an attorney instruct a deponent not to answer a question.[128]

In sum, depositions may be taken by written questions or oral examination, but most often are taken by oral examination for which the witness is subpoenaed. Written notice must be given to all the parties of the time and place for the deposition and of the identity of the deponent. Examination and cross-examination proceed as they would at trial, except that the testimony is taken following an objection. Professionalism conventions of civility and courtesy apply to the dialogue that takes place during a deposition.

J. Failure to Make Disclosures or Cooperate in Discovery

There are a variety of ways in which an attorney might violate the rules of discovery and, in particular, those rules specifically governing communications occurring as a part of discovery. Suffice it to say that failure to follow the Rules of Civil Procedure in these respects subjects both an attorney and her client to orders compelling disclosure or discovery, and the payment of attorney fees in conjunction with the opposing party's efforts to obtain such orders.[129] In addition, failure to comply with required discovery requirements may subject the attorney and her client to

---

125. *Id.* 30(b)(1).
126. *Id.* 45.
127. *Id.* 30(c)(2).
128. *Id.*
129. *Id.* 37(a).

sanctions.[130] In all events, the attorney should be aware that failure to conduct discovery communications in accordance with the Rules of Civil Procedure may result in adverse consequences.

IX. PRETRIAL MOTIONS

In filing pretrial motions, the attorneys communicate with one another and the court. The pretrial motion signifies an attorney's request for an order from the court.

When an attorney wants to obtain a court order, the proper method of communicating the request is by motion. A motion may be made during a hearing or trial, but otherwise must be in writing. The motion must specifically state the grounds for the motion and the relief sought by the motion.[131]

Additionally, "[t]he rules governing captions and other matters of form in pleadings apply to motions and other papers."[132] Thus, the motion must have a caption that identifies "the court's name, a title, a file number, and a Rule 7(a) designation."[133] In addition, pretrial motions must be signed by the attorney of record and identify the signer's address, e-mail address, and telephone number.[134] Again, conforming this type of submission to the rules of practice applicable in your jurisdiction is a form of professionalism.

There are a number of defenses that may be raised either by the responsive pleading or by pretrial motion, including lack of subject matter jurisdiction, lack of personal jurisdiction, improper venue, insufficient process, insufficient service of process, failure to state a claim upon which relief can be granted, and failure to join a party under Rule 19.[135] If the attorney wishes to raise these defenses by motion, rather than by responsive pleading, she must be certain to do so prior to filing the responsive pleading.[136] Some defenses are waived if not raised either by a motion prior to a responsive pleading or by responsive pleading, specifically, lack of personal jurisdiction, improper venue, insufficient process, and insufficient service of process.[137]

The Rules govern when other pretrial motions may be filed as well and the attorney should refer to Rule 12 of the Federal Rules of Civil Procedure to determine

---

130. *Id.* 37(d).

131. *Id.* 7(b)(1).

132. *Id.* 7(b)(2).

133. *Id.* 10(a).

134. FED. R. CIV. P. 11(a).

135. *Id.* 12(b).

136. *Id.*

137. *Id.* 12(h).

how to timely file a motion for judgment on the pleadings, a motion for more definite statement, a motion to strike, a motion for failure to state a claim upon which relief can be granted, a motion to dismiss for lack of subject matter jurisdiction, and a motion to join a person required by Rule 19(b). Complying with rules applicable to content and timing of such motions represents a professional discourse practice at the pretrial stage.

Which Is Worse—an Untimely Filing or Flyspecking Lawyers?

While a timely filing of documents is important to proper and professional communications, giving your opponent some latitude in timeliness is an equally important consideration of professional communications at the pretrial phase. In *Hyperphase Technologies, Inc. v. Microsoft Corporation*,[138] Microsoft electronically filed a motion for summary judgment at 12:04:27 a.m.—four minutes and twenty-seven seconds after the deadline. The U.S. Magistrate allowed the late filing and seemed more concerned with Hyperphase's inflexibility, noting that in spite of a previous order asking the parties not to "flyspeck" one another, at the sign of the late filing, nine of Hyperphase's attorneys immediately filed a motion to strike using bolded italics to make their point. The court stated "[w]ounded though this court may be by Microsoft's four minute and twenty-seven second dereliction in duty, [the court] will transcend the affront and forgive the tardiness. Indeed, to demonstrate the evenhandedness of its magnanimity, the court will allow Hyperphase on some future occasion in this case to e-file a motion four minutes and ***thirty*** seconds late . . . ." Sometimes communicating a courteous extension is more effective than pointing out your opponent's untimely filing.

---

138. No. 02-C-647-C, 2003 U.S. Dist. LEXIS 24345 (W.D. Wis. July 1, 2003).

5

TRIAL ADVOCACY

During a trial, there are many ethical and professional considerations regarding communications between attorneys and their clients, opposing counsel, jurors, judges, and witnesses. While most aspects of pretrial advocacy are addressed in Chapter 4, there are additional trial preparation procedures addressed here. In approaching the ethical and professional considerations related to communication at the trial level, consider the following stages.

I. TRIAL PREPARATION

There is a great deal to be done to prepare for trial, and communication is an essential component of that preparation. Trial preparation includes preparing the trial brief, which communicates the legal and factual basis of the claim and defense. In addition, trial preparation includes pretrial conferences, preparing clients and witnesses for trial, and meeting with clients in anticipation of trial. As with all representation, communication during trial preparation is governed by the Model Rules of Professional Conduct, which are specifically addressed in this chapter. Local rules of procedure also impose ethical and professional obligations on lawyers as they prepare for and conduct civil trials. In addition, you must be mindful of commonly understood conventions of professionalism, some of which are outlined here, (others are noted in Chapter 2). As noted in prior chapters, this manual addresses ethical and professional obligations related to civil trials. There are additional considerations for lawyers who try criminal cases, which are beyond the scope of this manual.

A. Preparation of the Trial Brief

In most cases, lawyers prepare trial briefs, or legal memoranda, for submission to the court. A trial brief is an "on the record" communication of the law and facts in support of the client's position that will be presented at trial. Trial briefs are subject to local rules and ethical rules. Key considerations when communicating in trial briefs are the *timeliness* of the communication, the *content* of the communication, and the *format* of the communication.

Trial briefs and legal memorandum are almost always subject to local rules, and those rules include considerations of timeliness, content, and format. For instance, many local rules provide specific requirements for communicating via a trial brief. These frequently include specific time requirements for when the opening and responding briefs must be filed prior to the trial. In addition, the rules often indicate required content, including statements of fact, references to admissions and stipulations of any applicable pretrial orders, and a summary of law with relevant legal citations. In addition to considerations of timeliness and content, the lawyer must also pay particular attention to local rules governing format, such as page limits, font, caption requirements, and the like.

The content of trial briefs is governed by the same ethical rules and court rules that apply to other types of court submissions. The Model Rules of Professional Conduct require that lawyers represent facts and legal positions honestly and accurately. First, Model Rule of Professional Conduct 3.3(a)(1) prohibits a lawyer from "knowingly mak[ing] a false statement of fact or law to a tribunal or fail[ing] to correct a false statement of material fact or law previously made to the tribunal by the lawyer." Further, Model Rule of Professional Conduct 3.3(a)(3) prohibits a lawyer from submitting false evidence. These rules not only require you to be truthful as to both the facts and law in your trial brief, but also to correct any errors, either legal or factual, you discover at a later time. Second, under Model Rule of Professional Conduct 3.3(a)(2), a lawyer is obligated to disclose authority in the controlling jurisdiction that is adverse to her client's position if opposing counsel has not disclosed it. This requires that your trial brief advise the court of controlling authority that opposes your legal position. Thus, these rules require that in preparing the trial brief, you should be certain to honestly portray the facts and to set forth the law, including law adverse to your client's case, accurately.

In addition to being truthful, Federal Rule of Civil Procedure 11 requires the attorney to conduct a reasonable inquiry of the facts and law. Federal Rule of Civil Procedure 11(b) provides:

> By presenting to the court a pleading, written motion, or other paper—whether by signing, filing, submitting, or later advocating it—an attorney or unrepresented party certifies that to the best of the person's knowledge, information, and belief, formed after an inquiry reasonable under the circumstances:
>
> (1) it is not being presented for any improper purpose, such as to harass, cause unnecessary delay, or needlessly increase the cost of litigation;
>
> (2) the claims, defenses, and other legal contentions are warranted by existing law or by a nonfrivolous argument for extending, modifying, or reversing existing law or for establishing new law;

(3) the factual contentions have evidentiary support or, if specifically so identified, will likely have evidentiary support after a reasonable opportunity for further investigation or discovery; and

(4) the denials of factual contentions are warranted on the evidence or, if specifically so identified, are reasonably based on belief or a lack of information.

Consequently, under Federal Rule of Civil Procedure 11, when you submit a trial brief to the court, you are certifying that you have made a reasonable inquiry into both the law and facts and that there is both sufficient evidentiary support of

---

Practice Pointer
What Constitutes Adverse Authority

In *Tyler v. State*,[1] a lawyer representing a client in a DWI matter failed to cite a prior decision of the Alaska Supreme Court, arguing that it was distinguishable from the matter before the court and therefore not controlling. The court disagreed with the lawyer's interpretation of the ethical obligation to disclose adverse authority, noting that the applicable ethics rule required citation to authority in the "controlling jurisdiction" where that authority was "directly adverse" to the client's position. The court emphasized the purpose of the rule—to protect the court and the proper administration of justice—noting

> The requirement that the authority be "directly adverse" has caused some problems of interpretation. Almost any adverse precedent can be distinguished . . . . Some might argue, therefore, that precedent which can be distinguished is not "directly" adverse and need not be revealed in the first place. This interpretation trivializes the rule and does not adequately protect the court.[2]

The court explained that, while a lawyer is obligated to represent client interests vigorously, that representation must be tempered by the lawyer's obligation of candor as an officer of the court. The best test, therefore, for whether a case should be cited is whether the court would consider the authority important, or would feel misled were the authority not revealed.

---

1. 47 P.3d 1095 (Ala. App. 2001)

2. *Id.* at 1106 (quoting GEOFFREY C. HAZARD & W. WILLIAM HODES, THE LAW OF LAWYERING (2nd ed. 1998)).

the facts and sufficient legal support of the legal claims and defenses. In addition, this certification communicates to the court that you are not asserting the brief for any improper purpose.

In sum, as you prepare a trial brief or responding briefs, be certain that your communication is timely filed. In addition, follow the local rules governing the particulars of format. Finally, be certain that you have made a reasonable inquiry of the facts and law so as to support the truthfulness of your communication of the facts and law set forth in the brief.

Practice Pointer
Trial Brief Checklist

Ensure that

✓ The trial brief and responsive briefs have been timely filed.

✓ The trial brief complies with technical requirements of local rules, such as font, margin, word limit, and content requirements.

✓ Facts are portrayed in a manner favorable to the client but thoroughly and accurately.

✓ Facts are supported by references to the record.

✓ Law is accurate and thorough.

✓ Quotations are accurate.

✓ Adverse authority has been cited and discussed.

✓ The brief has been reviewed for tone, paying attention to a proper characterization of opposing counsel's position.

B. Pretrial Conferences

Pretrial conferences are common in civil cases. The pretrial conference is intended to resolve some issues prior to trial. Typically, attorneys meet first to exchange witness lists and exhibits, negotiate stipulations and admissions, and to discuss the possibility of settlement. There may also be one or more formal meetings with the attorneys and the court prior to the trial. At this type of meeting the judge may rule on motions and clarify issues regarding procedure. At the close of this meeting one of the parties may draft a pretrial order that preserves the agreements and rulings rendered during the conference.

Practice Pointer

Iowa Form for Pretrial Order

I.C.A. Rule 1.1901-Form 6

Rule 1.1901-Form 6. Final Pretrial Order

IN THE IOWA DISTRICT COURT FOR _____ COUNTY

_____

No. _____

Plaintiff(s)

_____

         vs.   FINAL PRETRIAL ORDER

Defendant(s)

_____

FOLLOWING THE FINAL PRETRIAL CONFERENCE IT IS ORDERED:

1.   The following facts are undisputed: [list facts not in dispute]

2A. The following exhibits are received without objection:

2B. The following exhibits are subject to objection to be made at trial:

3.   The legal issues to be tried are: [list theories of recovery or defense]

4.   The factual issues to be tried are: [list the principal factual disputes and specifications of negligence or fault asserted by each party if applicable]

5.   Requested instructions, motions in limine, and trial briefs shall be filed by _____

6.   Trial will commence at _____ __.m. on _____

7.   It is further ordered that:

[list other matters the court desires to include]

Judge for the _____Judicial District of Iowa

Federal Rule of Civil Procedure 16 addresses pretrial conferences, noting a variety of purposes, including expediting disposition and/or maintaining control of the case, facilitating settlement, and improving the quality and efficiency of the proceedings. Matters that may be considered by the court include simplifying or dispensing with issues or claims; addressing evidentiary issues such as admissions, stipulations of fact, introduction of witnesses or documents; and controlling and scheduling discovery. The thorough, prepared lawyer will have carefully considered the types of issues that the court might consider at a pretrial conference.

Preparation may also include an investigation into the informalities of how a judge approaches pretrial conference dispositions. In *Attorney Grievance Commission of Maryland v. Milliken,*[3] a lawyer was sanctioned, in part, because he failed to appear at two previously scheduled pretrial conferences. The lawyer argued that he missed the first conference because of a scheduling error, and he missed the second because he had not checked his phone messages. In sanctioning the lawyer, the court noted that both the court and the client had a reasonable expectation that he would either appear at the conference or that he would give ample notice of his inability to attend. His failure to do either violated the ethical rules pertaining to diligent representation and the proper administration of justice. Thus, lawyers can be sanctioned for lapses in communication, including failure to communicate where such communication is expected or required.

Once the attorney has prepared for and attended the pretrial conference, an order will be entered setting forth the matters agreed upon in the pretrial conference. The form of the order may be set forth by local rule. Again, preparing a pretrial order is a form of written communication. The thorough, professional advocate will investigate and adhere to the required format of such a communication.

C. Communication with Witnesses

Pretrial communication with witnesses involves some issues of discovery addressed in Chapter 4. However, preparing for trial after discovery requires the lawyer to competently represent her client under the Model Rules which, in turn, includes the obligation to adequately prepare witnesses for trial. Preparing witnesses for trial necessarily requires an attorney to communicate with the witnesses about the content of the witnesses' testimony. There are, however, limitations and restrictions on the attorney's pretrial preparatory communications with witnesses. Pretrial preparation also requires the attorney to communicate with the witness about whether her participation is optional or required. Finally, considerations of professionalism require an attorney to consider what information ought to be communicated to the witness about what to expect at trial.

---

3. 704 A.2d 1225 (Md. 1998).

In order to adequately prepare for trial, a lawyer must communicate with a witness about the content of the witness's testimony. At this stage of the lawsuit, the lawyer will have conducted discovery and should have a fairly clear understanding of the witness's expected testimony. However, most lawyers want to spend time with the witnesses to communicate their expectations before trial. Indeed, courts have recognized the importance of this aspect of trial preparation:

> It is not improper for an attorney to prepare his witness for trial, to explain the applicable law in any given situation and to go over before trial the attorney's questions and the witness' answers so that the witness will be ready for his appearance in court, will be more at ease because he knows what to expect, and will give his testimony in the most effective manner that he can. *Such preparation is the mark of a good trial lawyer, and is to be commended because it promotes a more efficient administration of justice* and saves court time.[4]

During this pretrial preparation, the attorney often familiarizes the witness with the questions that will be asked at trial. The lawyer also reviews evidence and documents that may be relevant to or presented during the witness's testimony.

Meeting with witnesses prior to trial is also essential to reassure them about their participation in the trial process itself. There are a variety of things about a trial that are intimidating to nonlawyers, including the presence of the judge, jury, and court-room visitors. Witnesses are also anxious about the prospect of cross-examination. Lawyers should be respectful of the disruption to the witness's regular routine. In being a thoughtful lawyer, you should advise witnesses not only on the substance of their testimony, but also on other trial logistics, including timing considerations, where to park, and where to meet with the lawyer.

A lawyer's responsibility to prepare for trial—and to prepare witnesses—is tempered by ethical restrictions on *coaching* a witness. That is, there are professional limits on the content and purpose of your communication with witnesses for purposes of trial preparation. As noted by one scholar, there is a certain standard of ethical acceptability in witness coaching. First, a lawyer should feel free to discuss a case with witnesses before they testify and should also feel confident that she may "prepare witnesses so that they can deliver their testimony efficiently, persuasively, comfortably, and in conformity with the rules of evidence."[5] However, "when a lawyer discusses the case with a witness, the lawyer must not try to bend the witness's story or put words in the witness's mouth."[6] Finally, the rules of ethics prohibit the attorney from "counseling or assisting a witness to testify falsely or for

---

4. State v. McCormick, 259 S.E.2d 880 (N.C. 1979) (emphasis added).
5. Richard C. Wydick, *The Ethics of Witness Coaching*, 17 CARDOZO L. REV. 1 (1995).
6. *Id.*

knowingly offering testimony that the lawyer knows is false."[7] The two dangers of coaching are the inducement of false testimony and the possible "alteration of the witness's memory."[8] Essentially, the acceptable areas of communication with a potential witness are inquiries intended to uncover genuine facts and memories and those communications intended to provide the witness with information about the process of testifying.

As trial approaches, lawyers must notify witnesses whether their participation will be required. You do this by subpoenaing witnesses to ensure their appearance. This serves a variety of purposes. First, it protects the witness and provides an explanation for their presence at trial. Also, it protects the lawyer. In the event the witness does not appear, the subpoena preserves the lawyer's effort to secure the witness. Finally, the compulsion of appearance implicated by the subpoena may make the witness appear more impartial. Because a witness who receives a subpoena may be unfamiliar with these objectives, the professional lawyer will explain the purpose and objectives of the subpoena to the witness before she receives it.

D. Client Meetings

Clients are also often unfamiliar with judicial procedure and are frequently anxious about appearing in court. Thus, be sure to spend ample time with clients, apprising them with respect to the mechanics of the trial. As with other witnesses, the lawyer should review courtroom procedure and other details regarding trial, including parking and timing details. Clients should be given time to review their depositions, and they should be prepared for questions the lawyer intends to ask on direct examination as well as questions likely to be asked by opposing counsel on cross-examination. The lawyer's obligation as advisor under the Model Rules requires that the lawyer keep the client informed as to the status of the case, and requires the lawyer to give candid advice about the likelihood of success. While the division of responsibility places control of the objectives of representation with the client, the lawyer is responsible for the means of representation. A thorough explanation of the trial process, of the likelihood of success, and of the feasibility of settlement, are all necessary to enable the client to make informed decisions regarding representation.

E. Courtroom Decorum: Generally

Courtroom decorum relates to the manner in which lawyers observe rules, conventions, and expectations of professionalism in the courtroom. In some instances, the rules and conventions apply directly to how we communicate orally. In other instances, they pertain to how we subtly communicate our professionalism to the court and the courtroom participants through our physical presence in the courtroom.

---

7. *Id.*
8. *Id.* at 2.

Thus, trial communication includes familiarity with the courtroom and common procedures or conventions followed by the court and its participants. You should visit the courtroom prior to trial in order to become familiar with the layout of the courtroom, including the location of the bench and jury box, the counsel's table, the witness's chair, and the visitors' gallery. Further, you should have a familiarity with courtroom personnel, including the judge, clerk, reporter, bailiff, and other courtroom staff. All should be addressed and treated professionally as all are essential to the functioning of the system and, in many cases, to the lawyer's success in the courtroom. An increasing number of jurisdictions are adopting codes of professionalism that recognize the importance of civility to all participants in the judicial process, including courtroom personnel. As noted in the Code of Professionalism adopted by the San Diego Association of Business Trial Lawyers, Guideline 5:

> A lawyer should be punctual and prepared for all court appearances so that all matters may commence on the time and proceed efficiently. Lawyers should treat judges, counsel, parties, witnesses and court personnel on a civil and courteous manner, not only the court but in depositions, conferences and all other written and oral communications.[9]

So, lawyers are well-advised to treat all members of the staff with civility and respect.

Model Rule of Professional Conduct 8.4 addresses the obligations of a lawyer with respect to her communications with opposing counsel and witnesses. The rule prohibits conduct that is prejudicial to the administration of justice, including rude or disruptive behavior. *In Disciplinary Counsel v. LoDico,*[10] a lawyer was suspended for disruptive behavior, including speaking loudly at sidebars so that jurors could hear his comments and making dramatic facial expressions in front of the jury as witnesses testified. The court noted:

> The law demands that all counsel engender respect and dignity for the adjudication process. Though duty-bound to afford their clients the most competent representation of which they are capable, counsel are equally constrained by the mandates of integrity and professionalism imposed on all counsel as officers of the courts in which they appear. No proper defense or strategy warrants the type of misconduct exhibited by respondent . . . . We simply reinforce the mandate that our attorneys advocate within the rules of law, in the light of rational thought and reason rather than innuendo and incivility. Counsel must recognize that in every trial, the integrity of the process is as much at stake as are the interests of the accused. Justice must always appear just.[11]

---

9. http://www.abtl.org/sd_guidelines.htm (last visited April 23, 2009).

10. 833 N.E.2d 1235 (Ohio 2005).

11. Disciplinary Counsel v. LoDico, 833 N.E.2d 1235, 1241–42 (Ohio 2005) (citations omitted).

There have been a number of instances in which counsel have been repri-manded or sanctioned for misbehavior directed at opposing counsel. Such behav-ior is typically prohibited by codes of professionalism, which often include express prohibitions against ad hominum attacks and require courtesy and civility in com-munications between lawyers. In addition to express prohibitions, this behavior is strategically unwise as it undermines your integrity and credibility as an advocate with the jury.

Beyond following the relatively straightforward recommendation of civility in the courtroom, in order to be effective, a lawyer should be cognizant of the mechan-ics of delivering a successful argument. Having gained familiarity with the geogra-phy of the courtroom, you should pay attention to acoustics to ensure that your statements are audible to the court and members of the jury. Be sure that exhibits and other visual aids will be seen by the court and jury. Part of the lawyer's goal at trial is to engage the jury and keep their attention. As a thorough, professional lawyer, you should consider how the jury responds to information you offer, both visually and audibly.

In addition to obligations of civility in the courtroom, a professional lawyer will avoid excessive theatrics in the courtroom, as the "Dumb Shows" cautionary tale reveals.

The Model Rules of Professional Conduct obligate a lawyer to be truthful in addressing the court. This obligation extends beyond representations made directly by the lawyer to representations offered by witnesses the lawyer calls. Model Rule of Professional Conduct 3.3 prohibits a lawyer from making false statements of law or fact to the court. It also obligates lawyers to correct false statements previously made to the court. Under Rule 3.3, a lawyer may not

> offer evidence that the lawyer knows to be false. If a lawyer, the lawyer's client, or a witness called by the lawyer, has offered mate-rial evidence and the lawyer comes to know of its falsity, the lawyer shall take reasonable remedial measures, including, if necessary, disclosure to the tribunal. A lawyer may refuse to offer evidence, other than the testimony of a defendant in a criminal matter, that the lawyer reasonably believes is false.

These obligations continue through the conclusion of the proceeding. Thus, you should be constantly aware of the obligation of truthfulness and should adhere to it when addressing the court or any court-related personnel.

Cautionary Tale

Dumb Shows

R.J. Gerber writes:

Some lawyers take courtroom theatrics beyond the bounds of professionalism, using dramatic ploys, or dumb shows, designed to distract the attention of jurors. As one scholar explains:

> Some lawyers adopt wily silent ploys to distract judge and jury from important matters. Clarence Darrow employed one of the original "dumb" shows: he would insert a small wire into a lit cigar so that the jury's attention during his opponent's closing argument would be on the lengthening ashes which would almost, but never quite, fall.

Darrow's dumb show is by no means the most distracting nor offensive. A criminal defense attorney appeals to jury sympathy by arranging to have the defendant's small child crawl to him during closing argument. Here is the way the attorney describes this ploy:

> If the kid's a crawler, the best time to let him loose is during final argument. Imagine that little tyke crawling right up to you (make sure he comes to you and not the DA or, worse yet, the judge; a smear of Gerber's peaches around the cuff worked for me) while you're saying: "Don't strike down this good man, father to little Jimmy. Why Jimmy!" Pick the child up and give him to Daddy. If the DA objects and gets them separated, so much the better. Moses himself couldn't part a father and a son without earning disfavor in the eyes of the jury. Babies are truly miracles of life; they've saved many a father years of long-distance parenting. If your client's childless, rent a kid for trial.

There are infinite variations to this silent plea. In my own experience, I have seen a defendant approach the judge for sentencing while carrying a child to suggest that no one else is available to care for the child, who will be abandoned if a prison sentence is imposed.[12]

---

12. R.J. Gerber, *Victory vs. Truth: The Adversary System and Its Ethics*, 19 ARIZ. ST. L.J. 3, 15–16 (1987).

II. Jury Selection and Relations with Jurors

The mechanics of jury selection include consideration of who communicates with the jurors and how that communication is carried out. In some courts, particularly federal courts, voir dire is conducted by the judge with questions submitted by counsel. Other courts allow counsel to question jurors directly. In those jurisdictions procedural requirements may vary, with some courts requiring that counsel direct questions to the entire panel and other courts allowing members of the panel to be questioned individually. The professional advocate must familiarize herself with the requirements and procedures of the particular court.

There are generally two goals of jury selection. First, the attorney wants to identify and select jurors who will be most sympathetic to the client's position. Second, the attorney seeks to begin the process of persuading members of the jury to vote in favor of the attorney's client. Insofar as the goal of selecting a juror includes determining particular characteristics that might influence the juror's view of your client's case, you might include some personal questions in voir dire that are designed to elicit attitudes and potential biases. However, there are restrictions on the attorney's communications with the jurors.

With respect to ethical rules relating to communicating with jurors during jury selection, Model Rule of Professional Conduct 3.5 prohibits lawyers from seeking "to influence a judge, juror, prospective juror or other official by means prohibited by law." Further, under Model Rule of Professional Conduct 3.4, a lawyer may not

> allude to any matter that the lawyer does not reasonably believe is relevant or that will not be supported by admissible evidence, assert personal knowledge of facts in issue except when testifying as a witness, or state a personal opinion as to the justness of a cause, the credibility of a witness, the culpability of a civil litigant or the guilt or innocence of an accused.

The lawyer's objective in jury selection is to determine the attitude of prospective jurors regarding the client and his claim. However, communications proposing illegal influence are not allowed by the rules of ethics. Furthermore, you must also refrain from referring to facts that are not relevant or are unlikely to be supported by admissible evidence, as well as refrain from giving your personal opinion on a variety of matters. While voir dire is a time when you begin to persuade the jury, it is not intended for the presentation of evidence or attorney opinions.

In addition, when questioning the jury during voir dire, the lawyer should avoid questions that might unnecessarily embarrass potential jurors. Model Rule of Professional Conduct 4.4 prohibits a lawyer from use of "means that have no substantial purpose other than to embarrass, delay, or burden a third person." Common areas of acceptable inquiry include the following:

- Demographic questions, such as those involving the juror's occupation, marital and family status, and affiliation with organizations;

- Questions about the juror's familiarity with the law, including any bias against the legal doctrine that supports your client's claim;

- Questions involving people in the case;

- Questions involving experiences jurors have had that are similar to those involved in the case; and

- Questions as to whether jurors have actual knowledge about the facts of your client's case.

Consistent with other aspects of professional trial practice, avoid any attacks on opposing counsel. Finally, as with other aspects of trial, the competent, thorough lawyer will have detailed notes taken regarding the juror's responses to questions. A diagram of the jury panel is often helpful in this respect. Both of these practices will assist you in efficiently communicating with the potential jurors over the course of voir dire.

You are also advised to be polite and courteous to all members of the panel, but not overly ingratiating. In *Johnson v. Trueblood*, a lawyer's permission to appear pro hac vice was revoked, in part, because of his overly gratuitous communications with members of the jury—on a Friday afternoon of the trial, as the jury was dismissed, the lawyer smiled, waved, and told the jurors to "have a nice weekend."[13] Also, the court noted that the lawyer had been told by the judge that it was important for the court to recess at 4:00 because one of the jurors had a transportation issue. This information had been communicated privately to the lawyer. Notwithstanding, the lawyer later mentioned the issue in the presence of the jury, asking the court whether it intended to recess at 4:00 to accommodate the juror. The court revoked the lawyer's pro hac vice license, noting that his comments were unprofessional and designed to "gain special consideration" by the jury.[14] The revocation order was later vacated for failure to provide the lawyer the opportunity to respond to the allegations regarding unprofessional conduct. Notwithstanding, the case does reveal that, as with all other aspects of the trial, the lawyer's sincerity with respect to the client's position will be noted by the court and members of the jury and will affect how all respond to you and the argument you offer.

The following cautionary tale illustrates additional misconduct by an attorney during voir dire.

13. 476 F. Supp. 90, 96 (E.D.Pa. 1979), *vacated*, 629 F.2d 302 (1980).
14. *Id.*

Cautionary Tale
Misconduct During Voir Dire

In *Bardonner v. State,*[15] the court reversed a ruling and remanded for a new trial on the basis of comments made by the prosecutor during jury selection. During voir dire, the prosecutor endeavored to explain to the jury the respective roles of prosecutor and defense attorney. He stated (reading excerpts from Justice White's separate opinion in *U.S. v. Wade*)

The prosecutor "may prosecute with earnestness and vigor—indeed, he should do so. But while he may strike hard blows he's not at liberty to strike foul ones. It is as much his duty to refrain from improper methods calculated to produce a wrongful conviction as it is to use every legitimate means to bring about a just one."

Does that sound like the system that you would expect coming into the courtroom?

"Defense counsel need present nothing even if he knows what the truth is."

Again, that's in line with what I told you that he doesn't have any obligation to do anything. The burden is on the State of Indiana.

"He [defense counsel] need not furnish any witnesses to the police or reveal any confidences of his client, or furnish any other information to help the prosecution's case. *If he can confuse a witness, even a truthful one, or make him appear at a disadvantage, unsure or indecisive, that will be his normal course.*"

* * *

"Undoubtedly, there are some limits which defense counsel must observe but more often than not, defense counsel will cross-examine a prosecution witness, and impeach him if he can, even if he thinks the witness is telling the truth . . . .

"In this respect, as part of our modified adversary system and as part of the duty imposed on the most honorable defense counsel, we *countenance* or require conduct which in *many instances has little, if any, relation to the search for the truth.*"[16]

---

15. 587 N.E.2d 1353 (Ind. App. 4 Dist. 1992).

16. *Id.* at 1356 (quoting United States v. Wade, 388 U.S. 218 (1967) (emphasis added)).

The defense counsel objected, arguing that "to offer that language as an explanation to my role in this trial at this part of the proceeding has no purpose other than to prejudice this jury and to . . . establish [the Prosecutor's] position of being one of the Lone Ranger for truth and justice only and I am here to color the truth and alter the truth just like the previous argument that I argued against in a prior trial in this case. Now, that is improper, it is wrong, it is inflammatory, it is prejudicial." The trial court did not strike the comments and denied defense counsel's motion for a mistrial.[17]

On appeal, the appellate court reversed, finding prosecutorial misconduct on the basis of the comments made during voir dire. The court reasoned

> [T]he only purpose for the prosecutor's comments on the re-
> spective roles of defense and prosecution is to prejudice the
> jurors into viewing the prosecutor as a "good guy" and the
> defense counsel as a "bad guy." We think this is an unfair
> tactic which not only negates the defendant's presumption of
> innocence, but also runs afoul of Ind. Prof. Conduct Rule 3.4,
> which requires fairness to opposing party and counsel, and
> prohibits an attorney from alluding to matters that the lawyer
> does not reasonably believe are relevant or will not be sup-
> ported by the facts in issue. Here, the issue before the jury was
> whether the evidence was sufficient to convict the defendant
> of the crimes beyond a reasonable doubt. It is not the jurors'
> responsibility to make a finding as to the role of the prosecu-
> tor and defense counsel or to determine the character of the
> defense counsel. This information is certainly not relevant to
> the case.
>
> A defendant is entitled to a fair trial and an impartial
> jury. The import of the prosecutor's comments was to portray
> the defense counsel as *not* a decent, honorable person, but a
> shyster.[18]

---

17. *Id.* at 1356.

18. *Id.* at 1361 (internal citations omitted).

III. OPENING STATEMENT

Generally, the purpose of opening statement is to introduce the jury to the case and the evidence the lawyer intends to produce. Opening statement is not intended for argument or for a discussion of the law, both of which are typically prohibited.

Cautionary Tale

The Chummy Lawyer

In *Hawk v. Superior Court,*[19] a lawyer was held in contempt for, among other things, improperly referring to his friendship with his client. The lawyer was cautioned against such references but nevertheless included the following in his opening statement: "Okay. Let me tell you about the man that I smuggled cupcakes into his cell up in Yuba City on his birthday . . . contrary to the Sheriff's office regulations . . . [and] Let me tell you about Juan, the Christian." The opposing counsel objected to these comments.[20]

The court found the lawyer's references to his friendship and affection for the defendant, a "stubborn[] defi[ance of] the court's order to refrain from" such references. Holding the lawyer in contempt, the court noted that the references constituted improper and prejudicial attempts to influence the jurors, "a violation of the professional ethics . . . and an improper interference with the administration of justice and the trial of the case."[21]

In addition, Model Rule of Professional Conduct 3.4(e) prohibits a lawyer from alluding

> to any matter that the lawyer does not reasonably believe is relevant or that will not be supported by admissible evidence, assert[ing] personal knowledge of facts in issue except when testifying as a witness, or stat[ing] a personal opinion as to the justness of a cause, the credibility of a witness, the culpability of a civil litigant or the guilt or innocence of an accused . . . .

Thus, the lawyer should refrain from referring to evidence that the lawyer does not seriously believe will be admissible. Also, the rule prohibits a lawyer from acting as a witness or including personal opinions in the opening statements. Model Rule of Professional Conduct 3.4(c) prohibits a lawyer from "knowingly disobey[ing] an

---

19. 42 Cal. App. 3d 108 (1974).
20. *Id.* at 121.
21. *Id.* at 123.

obligation under the rules of a tribunal." Therefore, familiarity with and adherence to applicable rules is essential.

Practice Pointer

Impermissible material for opening statement:

- Do not allude to evidence that is inadmissible, that is, evidence that is likely to be excluded or evidence that cannot be produced. This is a professional obligation of the lawyer, as well as a strategic trial tactic. If evidence is promised in opening statements and not later produced at trial, jurors will remember the undelivered promise (particularly if opposing counsel chooses to remind jurors of the promise made during opening statement). Thus, you should avoid reference to evidence you do not reasonably believe will be admissible at trial.

- Avoid arguing during opening statement. If statements involve something the lawyer intends to—and can—prove at trial, they represent permissible statements.

- Be cautious with respect to any instruction regarding the law: It is the court's responsibility to instruct the jury as to the law. Therefore, it is not the responsibility of the advocate to argue the law during opening statement.

- Avoid any improper attempts to influence the jury.

- Avoid offering any personal opinions. The Model Rules of Professional Conduct prohibit counsel from asserting personal opinion regarding the case.

IV. EXAMINATION OF WITNESSES

A. General Considerations

Examination is the communication of the witness's testimony through a question and answer exchange between the attorney and the witness. Direct examination is the examination of the witnesses called on behalf of the attorney's client; cross-examination is the examination of witnesses called by opposing counsel. Some of the conventions of professionalism, evidentiary rules, and ethical rules apply to both direct and cross-examination.

You should refer back to the section on courtroom decorum to familiarize yourself with conventions of professionalism that govern courtroom communications. However, with respect to the process of witness examination specifically, you should be familiar with the particular procedure employed by the court to elicit testimony, whether that procedure is embodied in local rules or less formally understood as the practice of the particular court. In some courts, the judge prefers that counsel remain seated and question witnesses from counsel table or a lectern, while in other courts lawyers are free to walk around. Counsel should also be familiar with the rules and practices regarding the ability of the lawyer to approach the witness—in many jurisdictions lawyers may only do so with the permission of the court. In any event, requesting such permission is courteous and respectful of the court. Another aspect of procedure that is worth investigating is the manner in which the court prefers questioning. Many courts prefer specific questions and answers of a witness, rather than a long, narrative testimony.

Related to the idea of courtesy and respect in the process of examination of the witnesses is Model Rule of Professional Conduct 4.4, which prohibits a lawyer from employing "means that have no substantial purpose other than to embarrass, delay, or burden a third person." Courtesy and respect toward witnesses, both friendly and adversarial, are not only required by conventions of professionalism, but also to a certain extent by the rules of ethics.

Model Rule of Professional Conduct 3.4 provides that a lawyer may not knowingly disobey rules of court or allude to matters during trial that the lawyer does not reasonably believe will be supported by admissible evidence. Therefore, during examination of witnesses, this rule prohibits you from referring to inadmissible evidence, asserting personal knowledge of fact, or stating personal opinions. In addition, you are prohibited from asserting questions that violate any of the applicable rules of court. In terms of relevance and admissibility, the obligation is twofold: the lawyer should have a good faith *factual* and *legal* basis for the question.

The lawyer must not present perjurious testimony to the court. Under the Model Rule of Professional Conduct 3.3, a lawyer may not knowingly "offer evidence that the lawyer knows to be false." While the section below addresses this in the context of direct examination of the attorney's clients and witnesses, this prohibition against the presentation of false testimony is equally applicable during both direct and cross-examination. Because the prohibition only applies to evidence that the lawyer knows to be false, it is most likely to arise in the context of direct examination. You are, however, prohibited from eliciting testimony you know to be false on both direct and cross-examination.

B. Direct Examination

In addition to the above-noted conventions of professionalism and ethical rules applicable to all examination, there are evidentiary and ethical rules specifically applicable to direct examination.

When questioning witnesses on direct examination, you must generally avoid using leading questions. A leading question is one that suggests the answer to the question. Leading questions are permitted on cross-examination, but Federal Rule of Evidence 611(c) prohibits such questions on direct examination, "except as may be necessary to develop the witness' testimony." An attorney may also use leading questions on direct examination if the witness is "hostile" or is "an adverse party, or a witness identified with an adverse party."[22] As indicated by the notes to the federal rule, the suggestiveness of leading questions is what makes this type of questioning undesirable. The notes identify a variety of exceptions to the prohibition against leading questions, in addition to those noted within the rule itself, including questions directed to "[t]he witness who is hostile, unwilling, or biased; the child witness or the adult with communication problems; the witness whose recollection is exhausted; and undisputed preliminary matters."[23] As a practical matter, the determination of whether leading questions are appropriate for a particular witness or matter lies within the authority of the judge.

In addition to prohibitions against leading questions, lawyers are generally prohibited from eliciting testimony on direct examination that only serves the purpose of bolstering the credibility of the witness. However, lawyers routinely ask questions of witnesses designed to provide some background material about the witness, including education and occupation. Moreover, it is not improper to elicit testimony from a witness that is directly relevant to the credibility of the witness's testimony. What is improper is questioning designed to generally establish the witness's good character, lack of bias, or credibility. This information may only be elicited once the credibility of the witness has been questioned. Federal Rule of Evidence 608(a)(2) states that "evidence of truthful character is admissible only after the character of the witness for truthfulness has been attacked by opinion or reputation evidence or otherwise." The rationale behind this rule, as identified in *Lawrence v. State*,[24] is that the trier of fact has the responsibility of weighing the credibility of the parties and "that all witnesses are presumed to speak the truth, and may not be accredited until discredited by the evidence or otherwise, serves the process."[25] In sum, on direct examination, you may not ask questions to enhance your client's credibility unless her credibility has been attacked.

---

22. FED. R. EVID. 611(c)
23. *Id.* advisory committee cmt.
24. *Id.* 464 N.E.2d 923 (Ind. 1984).
25. *Id.* at 924 (internal citations omitted).

As noted in the earlier section addressing examination in general, under Model Rule of Professional Conduct 3.3(a)(3) a lawyer is prohibited from offering evidence that the lawyer knows to be false. This clearly prohibits the lawyer from eliciting testimony on direct examination that the lawyer knows to be false. The question is, what should you do if you know that the client intends to testify falsely or the client wants you to introduce the false testimony of another witness. The comments to the rule explain that in those situations, "the lawyer should seek to persuade the client that the evidence should not be offered. If the persuasion is ineffective and the lawyer continues to represent the client, the lawyer must refuse to offer the false evidence."[26]

The prohibition of introducing false evidence applies to information the lawyer *knows* to be false. Where the lawyer reasonably believes the material to be false, but has no knowledge of the falsity, and such knowledge cannot be inferred from the circumstances, the evidence should be admitted. The comments provide:

> A lawyer's reasonable belief that evidence is false does not preclude its presentation to the trier of fact. A lawyer's knowledge that evidence is false, however, can be inferred from the circumstances. Thus, although a lawyer should resolve doubts about the veracity of testimony or other evidence in favor of the client, the lawyer cannot ignore an obvious falsehood.[27]

Where a client or witness testifies falsely to the surprise of the lawyer, the rules impose an obligation on the lawyer to disclose the falsity to the court. When the lawyer does not know at the time of the testimony that it is false but later comes to know of it, Model Rule of Professional Conduct 3.3(a)(3) requires the lawyer to "take reasonable remedial measures, including, if necessary, disclosure to the tribunal." In addition, that rule provides that the "lawyer may refuse to offer evidence, other than the testimony of a defendant in a criminal matter, that the lawyer reasonably believes is false." Comment 10 speaks to the continuing obligation of the lawyer to take remedial measures to correct any false testimony offered. The comment advises that the lawyer should first consult with the client, then attempt to persuade the client to correct or withdraw the testimony. If the client will not cooperate, the lawyer may investigate whether withdrawal is permitted. If not, the lawyer is obligated to "make such disclosure to the tribunal as is reasonably necessary to remedy the situation, even if doing so requires the lawyer to reveal information that otherwise would be protected by Rule 1.6."[28] After that, it "is for the tribunal then to determine what should be done—making a statement about the matter to the trier of fact, ordering a mistrial or perhaps nothing."[29]

---

26. MODEL RULES OF PROF'L CONDUCT R. 3.3 cmt. 6 (2008).

27. *Id.* cmt. 8.

28. *Id.* cmt. 10.

29. *Id.*

The comments to Model Rule of Professional Conduct 3.3 recognize the implications of a lawyer's obligation to notify the court of false testimony by a client. While there may be serious consequences to the client, because the ultimate goal of any judicial proceeding is truth-finding, the lawyer's obligation remains to correct the falsity. The veracity of the attorney's communications with the court is paramount.

C. Direct Examination of Expert Witnesses: False Testimony

Model Rule of Professional Conduct 3.3 has particular implications when the lawyer is examining an expert witness on direct examination. The essential question—whether a lawyer has knowledge of the falsity of expert testimony—is complicated by the often technical nature of the testimony and the questions about methodology that are often inherent in the presentation of expert testimony. As noted earlier, while comment 8 to Rule 3.3 provides that a "reasonable belief that evidence is false does not preclude its presentation," that comment also states that the "lawyer cannot ignore an obvious falsehood," and a lawyer's knowledge of the falsity "can be inferred from the circumstances." What this likely means is that the lawyer must be reasonably diligent in ascertaining the truth of the expert witness's testimony. If the lawyer has been diligent in assessing the testimony, it is likely that the lawyer has fulfilled the obligation of proffering truthful expert testimony.

D. Cross-Examination

While cross-examination of witnesses does not occur until after presentation of the evidence on behalf of the client, which is dealt with below, it is included in this section because it is so closely related to direct examination of witnesses.

As an initial matter, the objective of the lawyer in terms of cross-examination should be put into perspective. While the goal of direct examination is to communicate proof of some material essential to the client's case, the goal of cross-examination is, generally, to discredit the material offered by the witness on direct examination or to limit its effect on the jury's decision-making. This is the most defensive aspect of trial and can therefore make it the most antagonistic. Abusive strategies designed to humiliate, embarrass, or harass a witness have no place in professional lawyering. The lawyer who puts excess energy into such abusive, defensive tactics would be well-advised to focus more attention and energy on her case-in-chief.

While leading questions are generally not permitted on direct examination, under Federal Rule of Evidence 611(c) they are "ordinarily" permitted on cross-examination. This conforms to tradition in making the use of leading questions on cross-examination a matter of right. The purpose of the qualification "ordinarily" is to furnish a basis for denying the use of leading questions when the cross-examination is cross-examination in form only and not in fact—for example, the "cross-examination" of a party by his own counsel after being called by the opponent, which more resembles re-direct.

Although mentioned earlier in the general section on examination, it is worthwhile to emphasize that Model Rule of Professional Conduct 4.4 prohibits a lawyer from using cross-examination to harass or embarrass a witness. On cross-examination, the lawyer is more likely tempted to employ sarcastic, argumentative, or degrading remarks or questions; nevertheless, the temptation should be avoided.

Practice Pointer
Objectives and Limitations of Cross-Examination

Federal Rule of Evidence 611 addresses the mode and order of interrogation. It states

(a) **Control by court.** The court shall exercise reasonable control over the mode and order of interrogating witnesses and presenting evidence so as to (1) make the interrogation and presentation effective for the ascertainment of the truth, (2) avoid needless consumption of time, and (3) protect witnesses from harassment or undue embarrassment.

(b) **Scope of cross-examination.** Cross-examination should be limited to the subject matter of the direct examination and matters affecting the credibility of the witness. The court may, in the exercise of discretion, permit inquiry into additional matters as if on direct examination.

(c) **Leading questions.** Leading questions should not be used on the direct examination of a witness except as may be necessary to develop the witness' testimony. Ordinarily leading questions should be permitted on cross-examination. When a party calls a hostile witness, an adverse party, or a witness identified with an adverse party, interrogation may be by leading questions.

There are additional considerations of professionalism that may arise in the course of cross-examination that are less likely to come up during direct examination. In terms of presenting a professional cross-examination, preparation is essential to maintaining control. Witnesses may evade a question or, at the other end of the spectrum, editorialize and explain their responses. There are a variety of ways to handle these issues, including asking the witness to limit responses to "yes" or "no," or asking the judge to instruct the witness or to strike the nonresponsive testimony. Familiarity with the court and the latitude the particular judge affords witnesses in responding is instructive when deciding the most effective technique to employ. As noted above, communicating with hostility or sarcasm is an unprofessional approach to controlling a wayward witness. Degrading a witness or attempting to confuse or distort testimony is neither ethical nor professional.

You should also anticipate interruptions during cross-examination. The judge has the discretion to interrupt cross-examination to request clarification or ask questions of the witness, and opposing counsel may object to a line of questioning. Expecting those interruptions is a part of trial preparation. Responding diplomatically as an advocate is a part of a professional discourse practice.

V. PRESENTATION OF EVIDENCE

There are a variety of procedural rules that govern the introduction and use of real and demonstrative evidence, including exhibits, photographs, charts, graphs, demonstrations, writings, and the like. For the purposes of this text, and the ethical and professional considerations associated with presentation of such evidence at trial, the lawyer should primarily keep in mind the restriction against alluding to materials that the lawyer does not believe will be supported by admissible evidence, and the corresponding obligation to avoid improper displays or sideshows in the courtroom. Materials should be presented with as little disruption as possible and with ample explanation and accessibility to enable the court and jury to appreciate the material. Dumb shows, as discussed above in the context of courtroom decorum, and other improper, unprofessional, or disruptive techniques should be avoided.

VI. TRIAL MOTIONS AND OBJECTIONS

Typically, an objection at trial is a communication by an attorney asking the court to exclude inadmissible evidence. Similarly, a lawyer may offer motions during trial to ask the court to rule on certain matters. The Model Rules of Professional Conduct require that competent lawyers be familiar with procedural rules relating to motions and objections and prohibit lawyers from asserting false or frivolous motions. For example, the rules on competence obligate lawyers to be familiar with procedure, which includes knowledge of how to make motions and objections at trial. As explained in the comments to Model Rule of Professional Conduct 3.1, the prohibition against advancing frivolous positions applies to motions.

Once a motion is made, the rules pertaining to the lawyer's obligation to further the proper administration of justice require that the lawyer properly yield to the rulings of the court on motions and objections. In *Hawk v. Superior Court*,[30] a lawyer

---

30. 42 Cal. App. 3d 108 (Cal. App. 1974).

was disciplined for remarks made when the court sustained a motion in favor of opposing counsel. Opposing counsel objected to questioning by attorney Hawk, arguing that his questioning of a witness went beyond the scope of direct examination. When the objection was sustained, attorney Hawk replied, "It is not beyond the scope of common sense."[31] The court found Hawk in contempt, finding that his refusal to yield to the ruling of the court constituted contempt.[32] This caution must be tempered with another important objective of the lawyer, preserving the record for appeal. This is also a proper activity of the lawyer in connection with her obligation to serve the interests of her client and can be best achieved with thoughtful motions and objections that, when made and ruled upon, are adhered to.

VII. CLOSING ARGUMENT

The closing argument is the lawyer's final communication to the fact finder and final attempt to persuade it to rule in favor of her client. Model Rule of Professional Conduct 3.3 prohibits a lawyer making false statements of law or fact. Model Rule of Professional Conduct 3.4 prohibits a lawyer from "knowingly disobey[ing] an obligation under the rules of a tribunal," and from stating "a personal opinion as to the justness of a cause, the credibility of a witness, the culpability of a civil litigant or the guilt or innocence of an accused." Therefore, it is improper to

- Distort facts by editorializing or embellishing testimony, alluding to facts beyond the record, or inviting speculation as to facts that have not been proven;

- Improperly distort the jury's consideration of the law by misstating or distorting legal standards or asking the jury to disregard some aspect of the law;

- Make emotional appeals to the jury by suggesting that they will be personally affected by the ruling or that their determination will be overturned by a higher court;

- Offer personal opinions as to the credibility of witnesses; or

- Attack opposing counsel's performance or credibility.

---

31. *Id.* at 131.

32. *Id.*

Practice Pointer

**Avoid Misleading
Statements and Personal Opinions**

In *Harne v. Deadmond*,[33] a lawyer had violated Model Rule of Professional Conduct 3.4 when he offered personal opinions about the credibility of witnesses during closing argument. The lawyer had identified himself to the jury as a former member of the state legislature. In his closing argument he tied this former legislative experience to a discussion of the law at issue. Opposing counsel objected, arguing that the lawyer had misstated the law. Indeed, during jury deliberations the jury sent back a question dealing with a misunderstanding of the law related to the lawyer's assertions during closing argument. The lawyer also told a lengthy story about his long-standing relationship with his client, in effect testifying about his experience with the client. The court ruled that these instances violated Rule 3.4:

> This Court has recognized the importance of Rule 3.4 in the context of a criminal proceeding. In *State v. Stringer*, we held that it is highly improper for the prosecutor to characterize either the defendant or witnesses as liars or offer personal opinions as to credibility. We recognized that when prosecutors make improper comments in the presence of the jury, "the prosecutor's personal views inject into the case irrelevant and inadmissible matters or a fact not legally proved by the evidence, and add to the probative force of the testimony adduced at the trial the weight of the prosecutors' personal, professional, or official influence." As a result, we warned, "this Court has been unequivocal in its admonitions to prosecutors to stop improper comment and we have made it clear that we will reverse a case where counsel invades the province of the jury . . . ." The same principles apply in the civil context when counsel, using the weight of his personal, professional, or official influence, improperly offers his opinion as to the justness of a cause or the credibility of a witness, particularly when the witness is his own client. Defense counsel's arguments to the jury in the present case violated the clear prohibition of Rule 3.4 and resulted in unfairness to the Harnes.[34]

---

33. 954 P.2d 732 (Mont. 1998).

34. *Id.* at 735 (internal citations omitted).

6

APPELLATE ADVOCACY

Communications at the appellate stage between attorneys and their clients, cocounsel, opposing counsel, and court personnel are similar in many respects to communications during trial. Obligations of competence, candor, and diligence remain applicable to attorney dialogue, both written and verbal. Additional considerations associated with rules of appellate procedure must also be considered.

In thinking about communications in the appellate process, consider the following stages:

I. PRE-APPEAL CONSIDERATIONS

A. Communicating with the Client before the Appeal

1. *Communications regarding representation*

You have an ethical duty to the client to explain whether you are in a position to represent the client during the appellate process. This will depend upon whether you are able to handle the appeal from a practical standpoint given the realities of your practice, and whether you are competent to represent the client through the appellate process.

2. *Communications regarding timing*

You must also advise the client as to any applicable timing considerations. At this stage, the most important time consideration is when you are required to file the notice of appeal. This is therefore a communication that is first made to the client, and then more formally to the court.

3. *Communications regarding the viability of the claim*

You must explain to the client whether there is a sufficient basis in both law and fact to support the issues to be raised on appeal, and the likelihood of success of the appeal. You also have an ethical and professional responsibility to explain other issues relating to the appeal, including, for example, the social and moral ramifications of filing an appeal. These communications implicate the allocation of responsibility between lawyer and client, with the client responsible for decisions involving the *ends* of representation and the lawyer responsible for decisions involving the *means* of representation.

B. The Notice of Appeal

The filing of the notice of appeal is the first formal communication of the appeal. The ethical and professional considerations associated with this form of communication relate to timing, format, and content.

C. Transmittal of the Record

In preparing and transmitting the record to the appellate court, the lawyer will likely communicate with opposing counsel and with the clerk of court. Again, the rules require the competent, responsible lawyer to be familiar with the rules of court applicable to this type of submission.

II. THE APPEAL

A. Appellate Briefs

The appellate brief is the most comprehensive, formal written communication of the appeal. Court rules related to format, content, and timing must be observed. In addition, ethical rules address content considerations of accuracy and candor. Finally, conventions of professionalism with respect to how the opposing position is considered should be observed.

B. Appeal Conferences

During appeal conferences the lawyer will communicate with opposing counsel and the court. She may also communicate with the client prior to and following the conference. Rules relating to the objectives of these conferences should be considered, as well as expectations of professionalism, civility, and courtesy.

C. Oral Argument

Oral argument is the lawyer's opportunity to engage in a formal discussion with the court. There are several ethical and professional considerations associated with this form of communication.

D. The Judgment

Once the judgment is rendered by the appellate court, the lawyer will communicate with his client and must explain the disposition and any remaining alternatives to the client.

III. POST-APPEAL CONSIDERATIONS

A. Post-Opinion Motions

The party who loses the appeal may file a Motion for Rehearing.

B. Petitions for Certiorari

The party that lost the appeal may file a petition for certiorari to a higher appellate court that has the discretion to grant or deny the appeal.

This chapter specifically addresses appellate advocacy; however, you should continue to consider how the general rules and conventions of professionalism as described in Chapter 2 impact communication during the appellate process.

I. PRE-APPEAL CONSIDERATIONS

A. Communicating with the Client before the Appeal

At this stage in the appellate process, much of the communication will be between lawyer and client. When a trial has concluded and a judgment has been rendered, the party that lost at the trial level may consider filing an appeal. The lawyer who is asked to represent a client on appeal must first consider whether she is in a position to represent the appellate party. She must determine whether she has the level of competence necessary to address not only the issues on appeal, but also the appellate rules of procedure. The lawyer is also responsible for determining whether there are viable issues for appeal and for communicating that viability to the client so that the client can determine whether to proceed with the appeal. Model Rule of Professional Conduct 1.2 allocates responsibility for decisions regarding representation. Under this rule the client has the ultimate responsibility for decisions regarding the ends of representation, while the lawyer has the responsibility for decisions regarding the means to accomplish those ends. This allocation of responsibility raises issues of professionalism with respect to the communication between lawyer and client. Under Model Rule 1.4(b), in order to enable the client to make reasoned decisions regarding the objectives of representation, including objectives associated with an appeal, the lawyer must "explain a matter to the extent reasonably necessary to permit the client to make informed decisions regarding the representation." In terms of this responsibility, as a lawyer you must be candid about not only the appellate process and the merits of the client's position, but also about the implications of protracted litigation.

As an initial matter, then, the lawyer representing the losing party at the trial level must examine the viability of the appeal and communicate his advice to the client. There are several things to consider in this regard, including applicable filing dates, whether potential errors for appeal have been adequately preserved in the record, and the extent to which the standard of appellate review applicable to the appealable issue undermines the likelihood of a successful appeal. As each of these issues impact the advice communicated to the potential appellate client, each merits a brief discussion.

Communications Regarding Representation

In assessing the appeal, the competent lawyer should be careful to examine the trial court judgment. Only final judgments may be appealed. Where the judgment disposes of fewer than all parties or claims, it may not be final for purposes of appellate jurisdiction. Further, the appellate lawyer must carefully examine the record to determine whether an error has been adequately preserved for appeal. Evidentiary and procedural errors are typically preserved by objection at trial or by an adequate offer of proof. To the extent the appeal involves particularly sophisticated or complex legal issues, or issues outside the expertise of the lawyer, the rules on competency recommend seeking the assistance of a seasoned appellate lawyer: "Competent representation can also be provided through the association of a lawyer of established competence in the field in question."[1]

Communications Regarding Timing

In addition to assessing whether the substantive matter is appropriate for an appeal, a competent lawyer must also establish filing dates relevant to the appeal, and these will impact the timing of communication to the client and the court. Generally, the appellant must file a notice of appeal within a certain time frame. This typically begins to run from the entry of the trial court's judgment. Sometimes a lawyer represents a party at the trial and the appellate court level. Other lawyers specialize in appeals. An initial consideration therefore, particularly when the appellate lawyer represents a new client seeking an appeal, is whether time has run on the ability to file the notice of appeal. For the lawyer representing the losing party at the trial court level, this timing consideration should be communicated to the losing party in order to preserve the opportunity to file an appeal, if viable. Filing deadlines vary by jurisdiction and also according to the type of decision being appealed. They can be as short as ten days (for an appeal from a federal criminal judgment) to thirty days. A failure to meet the applicable deadline for filing an appeal is rarely excused, sometimes with disastrous consequences for lawyers and their clients. For example, in *Coleman v. Thompson*,[2] the U.S. Supreme Court upheld a capital sentence after a lawyer filed an appeal from the denial of a state habeas petition. The filing deadline for the appeal was thirty days. The appeal was filed on the thirty-third day. Because it was late, the appeal was denied and the death sentence was upheld.

Communications Regarding the Viability of the Claim

In examining the record for an appealable issue, the lawyer must also establish that there is a good-faith basis in the law and facts supporting the appeal. Model Rule of Professional Conduct 3.1 provides: "A lawyer shall not bring or defend a proceeding, or assert or controvert an issue therein, unless there is a basis in law and fact for doing so that is not frivolous, which includes a good faith argument for an extension, modification or reversal of existing law." A related obligation exists in the Federal Rules of Appellate Procedure, which prohibit lawyers from filing frivolous briefs. While these preliminary determinations do not implicate communication per se, they are related to both the communicative advice the lawyer will provide to the client regarding the viability of the appeal and, in the event an appeal is filed, to the communicative materials made in the context of appellate advocacy. These are discussed more fully later in this chapter.

---

1. MODEL RULES OF PROF'L CONDUCT R. 1.1 cmt. 2 (2008).
2. 501 U.S. 722 (1991).

Finally, in assessing the viability of an appeal and communicating the likelihood of success to the client, a good lawyer should objectively consider the standard of appellate review applicable to the issue being raised on appeal. A discussion of appellate standards of review is beyond the scope of this text, but it is important to note that, if the standard of review is highly deferential to the trial court's ruling, the likelihood of success on appeal is diminished. This should correspondingly influence the lawyer's candid advice to the client about the viability of her appeal.

Cautionary Tale

Nonfrivolous Basis in Law and Fact

In *In re Zimmerman*,[3] a lawyer, Zimmerman, was sanctioned, in part, for his failure to have a good-faith basis for an issue raised on appeal. Zimmerman filed an action on behalf of his client against General Motors, claiming that the client had been injured in a car accident and that the injuries were due to a defect in the car's seat belts. During discovery General Motors produced an affidavit from an expert who concluded that the seat belts were not defective. General Motors filed a Motion for Summary Judgment, which was granted. Zimmerman then filed a late notice of appeal of the issue, which was dismissed. In a disciplinary hearing on the matter, Zimmerman testified that he did not respond to the Motion for Summary Judgment because he did not believe that he had a good-faith basis to do so. The disciplinary panel concluded that he therefore could not have had a good-faith basis to appeal the court's order granting the motion. This case represents a failure in communication at two levels. First, the lawyer should have fully explained the impact of the adverse summary judgment to the client, who might well have foregone the appeal. Moreover, the lawyer's filing of the appeal constituted a frivolous filing at the appellate level, and therefore a communication to the court that ran afoul of the ethical rules.

Thus, in terms of communicating either verbally or in writing with clients, the lawyer must recognize that while the client may be disappointed by the outcome at trial, a critical examination of the merits of the appeal is an ethical obligation of the lawyer. Therefore, if the time for filing has run, or if there is no viable basis for appeal, you have an obligation to be candid with the client and reject the filing of an appeal. In fact, Model Rule of Professional Conduct 2.1 imposes upon the lawyer an obligation to deliver bad news to a client, which may include the lawyer's lack of confidence in an appeal.

---

3. 19 P.3d 160 (Kan. 2001).

> ### Practice Pointer
> ### The *Anders* Brief and Appointed Counsel's Right to Withdraw
>
> The lawyer's duty to represent clients effectively on appeal can become complicated in cases where the lawyer is appointed to represent an indigent client on an appeal as of right. In some instances, the lawyer may conclude that because there are no arguable issues for appeal any claim made on appeal would be frivolous. In *Anders v. California*,[4] the U.S. Supreme Court addressed the ethical obligations of the lawyer to protect the indigent client's constitutionally protected rights. The Court concluded that in an instance where the appointed lawyer determines that there are no meritorious issues for appeal, the lawyer is obligated to review the record and prepare a brief that addresses any arguable issues for appeal. This brief should be provided to the court and to the client. The court would then be in a position to review the record, focusing on any arguable issues raised by the lawyer, to confirm the lawyer's analysis and enable the lawyer to withdraw from representation. The Court explained
>
>> This requirement would not force appointed counsel to brief his case against his client but would merely afford the latter that advocacy which a nonindigent defendant is able to obtain. It would also induce the court to pursue all the more vigorously its own review because of the ready references not only to the record, but also to the legal authorities as furnished it by counsel. The no-merit letter, on the other hand, affords neither the client nor the court any aid. The former must shift entirely for himself while the court has only the cold record which it must review without the help of an advocate. Moreover, such handling would tend to protect counsel from the constantly increasing charge that he was ineffective and had not handled the case with that diligence to which an indigent defendant is entitled. This procedure will assure penniless defendants the same rights and opportunities on appeal—as nearly as is practicable—as are enjoyed by those persons who are in a similar situation but who are able to afford the retention of private counsel.[5]
>
> In later Supreme Court rulings, the Court reinforced the dual objectives of the *Anders* brief: to enable the appellate court to determine that appointed counsel had fulfilled her duty to support the client's appeal to the best of her ability and to afford the appellate court the opportunity to make its own determination that an appeal would indeed be frivolous.

4. 386 U.S. 738 (1967).

5. *Id.* at 744–45.

Also, in discussing an appeal with a client, you should be candid with the client regarding the costs—financial and otherwise—of protracted litigation. Model Rule of Professional Conduct 2.1 notes: "In representing a client, a lawyer shall exercise independent professional judgment and render candid advice. In rendering advice, a lawyer may refer not only to law but to other considerations such as moral, economic, social and political factors that may be relevant to the client's situation." The comments explain that purely legal advice may be inadequate to a client:

> Advice couched in narrow legal terms may be of little value to a client, especially where practical considerations, such as cost or effects on other people, are predominant . . . .[6]

> A client may expressly or impliedly ask the lawyer for purely technical advice . . . . When such a request is made by a client inexperienced in legal matters, however, the lawyer's responsibility as advisor may include indicating that more may be involved than strictly legal considerations.[7]

While this rule is rarely enforced as a disciplinary matter, you are advised to be cognizant of the financial and emotional stress of continuing litigation and should therefore communicate candidly with the client regarding these matters. Indeed, the professional lawyer should be candid with the client regarding all implications of the appeal, including the additional costs associated with protracted litigation. As the court acknowledged in *In re Marriage of Pitulla*[8]

> We believe that in every contract for hire between an attorney and his client, there is implied in the contract the client's right to always know what the attorney did or does, and how much time he took to do it. The time-honored ideals of the legal profession and the continuing need for public confidence in the legal profession demand this conclusion.[9]

Note that this obligation is in addition to your responsibility to clearly communicate with the client regarding the legal issues and technical viability of a successful appeal.

B. The Notice of Appeal

During this stage of the appeal, the lawyer will communicate with the trial court as well as the opposing counsel. The notice of appeal is a formal communication,

---

6. MODEL RULES OF PROF'L CONDUCT R. 2.1 cmt. 2 (2000).

7. *Id.* cmt. 3.

8. 491 N.E.2d 90 (Ill. App. Ct. 1986)

9. *Id.* at 94.

made to the court and opposing counsel, of the intent to file an appeal. The primary issues that arise in this context include those of the timing, content, and format of the communication. One of the primary ethical obligations of the lawyer at this stage is to be familiar with the appellate court rules and to be diligent regarding filing deadlines. Model Rule of Professional Conduct 1.3 requires that a lawyer "act with reasonable diligence and promptness in representing a client." Further, Model Rule of Professional Conduct 3.2 requires that a lawyer "make reasonable efforts to expedite litigation consistent with the interests of the client." To that end, the rules note the importance of meeting deadlines and avoiding unreasonable delay. Thus, to ensure competent, diligent representation, you should understand the local rules applicable to filing the notice of appeal. There are strict deadlines for

---

Cautionary Tale

Failure to Timely File Notice of Appeal and Excusable Neglect Professionalism Precludes Passing the Buck

Lawyers are busy people, and law offices typically handle heavy client workloads. These burdens, however, will rarely excuse a lawyer's failure to meet an applicable filing deadline. For example, in *In re Boggs*,[10] a bankruptcy lawyer failed to file a timely notice of appeal. He argued that when the order sought to be appealed was received in his office, the person responsible for the mail was out sick. Further, he argued, the person in the office responsible for docketing the deadline was out of the office. The court rejected the lawyer's argument that these ministerial mishaps amounted to excusable neglect, noting, "[w]here counsel have attempted to convince courts that deadlines missed through mistakes made by office staff or by other pressures associated with the operation of a legal practice were the result of excusable neglect, they have been soundly rebuffed."[11] The lawyer appealed this determination and a panel of the Sixth Circuit affirmed, reinforcing that"'[c]lerical or office problems' are simply not a sufficient excuse for failing to file a notice of appeal within the ten day period."[12] Thus, even if the lawyer delegates administrative duties to a member of her staff, she remains responsible for the client file, including filing deadlines. Communications to the court that blame office staff for failures in the lawyer's responsibility are unprofessional and, as the case illustrates, unlikely to be persuasive.

---

10. 246 B.R. 265 (Bankr. 6th Cir. 2000).

11. *Id.* at 267.

12. *Id.*

filing the notice of appeal, and most jurisdictions have specific rules regarding the content and format of the notice. Under the Federal Rules of Appellate Procedure, the notice of appeal must identify the parties taking the appeal, the judgment or order appealed from, and the court to which the case is being appealed. For certain matters, additional case information forms may be required. The other parties to the judgment may then be notified of the appeal by the clerk of the court from which the matter was appealed, or the appellant may be required to serve notice of the appeal on the opposing party. A competent, responsible lawyer must familiarize herself with the procedural aspects of initiating the appeal in order to ensure professional communication and practice.

In most jurisdictions an appealing party may be given leave to file a late notice of appeal. To obtain leave to file a late notice, the appellant must file a motion for a special order granting a late notice with the *appellate* court. The appellate court may issue the special order upon the motion, with notice to the adverse parties, and on a showing by affidavit or otherwise that the delay was not due to the appellant's culpable negligence. When a special order is granted, the clerk of the trial court may allow the filing of a notice of appeal within the time specified by the appellate court.

C. Transmittal of the Record

The transmittal of the record is a form of communication by the appellate lawyer, and she must be familiar with any filing requirements so as to adequately protect the interests of her client on appeal. Under the Federal Rule of Appellate Procedure 10(b), the appellant is required to order the trial transcript from the reporter and, if the entire transcript is not to be included in the record, to serve a statement of the issues the appellant intends to present on appeal. While in most cases the clerk of the trial court has the responsibility for transferring the record, it is essential that all appellate lawyers be familiar with local filing rules. Local rules, which vary by jurisdiction, may require that specific content be delivered to the appellate court. Further, with respect to the logistics of transferring the record, there may be local variations. In some cases the appellant bears the burden of transmitting exhibits or additional documents to the appellate court.

II. THE APPEAL

A. Appellate Briefs

There are many ethical and professional considerations that apply to the content and form of appellate briefs. Timely filing and compliance with local rules regarding format are essential for the attorney to enjoy a professional reputation before the court. Adherence to ethical rules regarding candor and competence require that the legal and factual representations in the brief be well-supported. Finally, to support the credibility and ethical reputation of the advocate, the tone of the brief should be professional, avoiding disparaging comments about the lower court's ruling, opposing counsel, or the opposing parties. Because an appellate brief is a written communication to the court, you are advised to follow the general considerations for written communication outlined in Chapter 2. The first thing the professional lawyer does when preparing to write an appellate brief is to locate the local rules that address the appellate brief and familiarize herself with all the requirements contained in those local rules. Adherence to formatting requirements, as well as conforming the content of the appellate brief to ethical and procedural requirements, constitutes a form of professional communication.

Like trial briefs at the trial or district court level, an appellate brief is an "on the record" communication of the law and facts in support of the client's position that will be presented at trial. Appellate briefs are subject to both procedural as well as ethical rules. Key considerations of communicating in appellate briefs are the *timeliness* of the communication, the *content* of the communication, and the *format* of the communication.

Appellate briefs are subject to local rules, and those rules include considerations of timeliness, content, and format. For instance, many local rules of appellate courts provide specific requirements for communicating via a trial brief. These frequently include specific time requirements within which the opening and responding briefs must be filed prior to the appeal. In addition, the rules often indicate required content, including statements of fact, issues raised on appeal, and references to the lower court ruling and appellate record. In addition to considerations of timeliness and content, the lawyer must also pay particular attention to local rules governing format, such as page limits, font, caption requirements, and the like.

The content of appellate briefs is governed by the same ethical rules and court rules that apply to other types of court submissions. The Model Rules of Professional Conduct require that lawyers represent facts and legal positions honestly and accurately. First, Model Rule of Professional Conduct 3.3(a)(1) prohibits a lawyer from "knowingly mak[ing] a false statement of fact or law to a tribunal or fail[ing] to correct a false statement of material fact or law previously made to the tribunal by the lawyer." Further, Model Rule of Professional Conduct 3.3(a)(3) prohibits a lawyer from submitting false evidence. These rules not only require you to be truthful as to both the facts and law in your appellate brief, but also to correct any errors, either legal or factual, if you discover them at a later time. While the appellate practitioner's objective is to persuade the court to rule in favor of his client, the lawyer's obligation as an officer of the court is to assist the appellate court in resolving the matter appropriately in light of the law and facts of the dispute. Most court rules addressing the facts section of briefs require that all references to facts be supported by citations to the record. Federal Rule of Appellate Procedure 28(a)(7) requires that an appellate brief include "a statement of facts relevant to the issues submitted for review with appropriate references to the record." Adhering to these requirements not only satisfies the rule but also enhances your credibility with the appellate court. Further, if you include a fact in the appellate brief that is not supported by the record, you damage your credibility with the court to the extent that none of your arguments may be persuasive.

Cautionary Tale

Importance of a Well-Prepared Argument

It should be obvious that the lawyer has an obligation to the client to prepare a well-written brief. There is also an obligation to the court and to the administration of justice, as the court aptly noted in *Smith v. Town of Eaton*.[13] In *Smith*, the appellate lawyer was fined for filing what the court described as a "rambling, almost totally incomprehensible" brief.[14] The court noted that the rules of appellate procedure require lawyers to prepare professional briefs. The court then described the impact of a failure in this regard:

> Unprofessional presentation of arguments not only is a disservice to this court, but also "is a disservice to other litigants," who must wait while this court is forced to undertake the extra duty of formulating counsel's arguments. Especially now, when the court system is burdened to capacity, and when judicial resources are stretched to the very limit, our fiduciary duty to the institution we serve and to *all* the litigants who come before us requires that we be vigilant in enforcing the bar's responsibility to present issues clearly and comprehensively.[15]

With respect to crafting the legal argument in an appellate brief, there are also some ethical and professional considerations to consider. While this is not a text that endeavors to explain the process of effective analytical persuasion in the form of an appellate brief, there are several issues worth mentioning in the context of preparing an effective, professional legal argument section for an appellate brief. First, make the court's job as easy as possible. Provide accurate references to authority and to the record. This is typically a requirement under the applicable appellate rules, as Federal Rule of Appellate Procedure 28 requires that an appellate brief contain "appellant's contentions and the reasons for them, with citations to the authorities and parts of the record on which the appellant relies." Indeed, few things undermine the

---

13. 910 F.2d 1469 (7th Cir. 1990).

14. *Id.* at 1470.

15. *Id.* at 1470–71.

credibility of a lawyer more than misrepresentations with respect to the law or the facts.

Pay attention to the form of the document, and make it accessible to the reader. Outline the legal argument before you begin writing, and focus your attention on the primary issues. Many lawyers make the mistake of trying to address too many minor issues. While this is not necessarily unethical or unprofessional, it rarely results in effective advocacy. Finally, be sure to represent the law accurately. While you may ask the court to consider a broad application of a prior ruling, do so openly. For example, under Model Rule of Professional Conduct 3.3(a)(2), a lawyer is obligated to disclose authority in the controlling jurisdiction that is adverse to the client's position if opposing counsel has not disclosed it. This requires that your appellate brief advise the court of controlling authority that opposes your legal position. Thus, these rules require that in preparing the appellate brief, you should be certain to honestly portray the facts and to set forth the law, including law adverse to your client's case, accurately.

In addition to being truthful, Federal Rule of Civil Procedure 11 requires the attorney to conduct a reasonable inquiry of the facts and law. Federal Rule of Civil Procedure 11(b) provides:

> By presenting to the court a pleading, written motion, or other paper—whether by signing, filing, submitting, or later advocating it—an attorney or unrepresented party certifies that to the best of the person's knowledge, information, and belief, formed after an inquiry reasonable under the circumstances:
>
> (1) it is not being presented for any improper purpose, such as to harass, cause unnecessary delay, or needlessly increase the cost of litigation;
>
> (2) the claims, defenses, and other legal contentions are warranted by existing law or by a nonfrivolous argument for extending, modifying, or reversing existing law or for establishing new law;
>
> (3) the factual contentions have evidentiary support or, if specifically so identified, will likely have evidentiary support after a reasonable opportunity for further investigation or discovery; and
>
> (4) the denials of factual contentions are warranted on the evidence or, if specifically so identified, are reasonably based on belief or a lack of information.

Consequently, under Federal Rule of Civil Procedure 11, when you submit an appellate brief to the court, you are certifying that you have made a reasonable inquiry into both the law and facts and that there is both sufficient evidentiary support for the facts and sufficient legal support of the legal claims and defenses made on appeal. In addition, this certification communicates to the court that you are not asserting the brief for any improper purpose.

Cautionary Tale
Bad Manners and a Lawyer's Reputation

Courts have not been reluctant to criticize lawyers for unprofessional language in briefs. In *Advanced Restoration, L.L.C. v. Priskos*,[16] the court criticized a lawyer for hyperbole in a brief, specifically citing the following language as inappropriate: the brief's statement "that both Landlord and Tenant 'ought to be ashamed of themselves,' and repeatedly refer[ing] to opposing counsel's arguments as 'revolting,' 'disingenuous,' 'nonsensical,' 'insulting to the intelligence of the Court,' 'ridiculous,' and 'reprehensible.'" The court then stated

"Derogatory references to others or inappropriate language of any kind has no place in an appellate brief and is of no assistance to this court in attempting to resolve any legitimate issues presented on appeal."[17] We also remind counsel that, as lawyers, they are bound by the Rules of Professional Conduct, which require lawyers to maintain the decorum of the tribunal, and that "refraining from abusive or obstreperous conduct is a corollary of the advocate's right to speak on behalf of litigants."[18] Additionally, the Standards of Professionalism and Civility, promulgated by the Utah Supreme Court, urge lawyers to "avoid hostile, demeaning, or humiliating words in written and oral communications with adversaries."[19] Finally, we advise counsel that appellate briefs must be free from "burdensome, irrelevant, immaterial, or scandalous matters. Briefs which are not in compliance may be disregarded or stricken, on motion or sua sponte by the court, and the court may assess attorney fees against the offending lawyer."[20]

---

16. 126 P.3d 786, 797 (Utah Ct. App. 2005).

17. *Id.* (quoting State v. Cook, 714 P.2d 296, 297 (Utah 1986)).

18. *Id.* (quoting UTAH R. PROFESSIONAL CONDUCT 3.5 cmt.).

19. *Id.* (quoting UTAH STANDARDS OF PROFESSIONALISM AND CIVILITY 3).

20. *Id.* (quoting UTAH R. APP. P. 24(j)).

In order to ensure a professional communication in your appellate brief, you should also pay attention to tone. You will lose credibility by referring to the lower court's ruling disrespectfully, and the loss of credibility may impact your client's position. While it is appropriate to challenge the basis for the ruling, it is unprofessional to attack the court's intelligence. It is similarly unprofessional (and may impact counsel's credibility) to include personal attacks on opposing counsel or the opposing party. Finally, avoid excessive language and hyperbole—this undermines credibility. Characterizing circumstances as "outrageous" and arguments as "wholly without merit" is not effective. Moderation and courtesy in tone go a long way in establishing a professional reputation. In contrast, effective legal arguments are obscured by personal attacks and excessive, disrespectful criticism of the lower court's decision. Indeed, many judges have acknowledged that personal attacks undermine the integrity of the argument. As one judge notes:

> We all know the old adage: If the law is with you, argue the law; if the facts are with you, argue the facts; if neither is with you, call the other guy names. As soon as I see an attack of any kind on the other party, opposing counsel, or the trial judge, I begin to discount the merits of the argument.[21]

Judge Saufley recommends that briefs be focused, absolutely accurate, and accessible to the reader.[22]

Finally, the ethical and professional appellate brief will conform to applicable format requirements. Most courts have strict guidelines on format for appellate briefs, including rules addressing page size; typeface style and size; spacing; page, line, or word limits; and, in some cases, paper quality. Briefs also typically have color-coded covers, with different colored covers identifying the appellant's brief on the merits, the respondent's brief on the merits, the appellant's second briefs in cross-appeals, amicus' briefs, etc. There are additional rules that address electronic filing of briefs and the need in some cases for the filing of a CD-ROM or disk of the brief.

While format requirements may not appear to implicate issues of ethical and professional communication, they have an enormous impact. The Model Rules impose an obligation upon lawyers to be familiar with and comply with format requirements—this is an aspect of competence addressed in Model Rule 1.1, which requires lawyers to use "methods and procedures meeting the standards of competent practitioners."[23] To ensure the requisite level of competence in appellate practice, including competence with respect to procedure, lawyers with limited experience may need to associate with an experienced appellate practitioner. In

---

21. Leigh Ingalls Saufley, *Amphibians and Appellate Courts*, 50 ME. L. REV. 18, 22 (1999).
22. *Id.*
23. MODEL RULES OF PROF'L CONDUCT R. 1.1 cmt. 5 (2008).

terms of preparation, appellate work differs from trial work in certain respects. To the extent the rules of competence require a standard of thoroughness and preparation, the lawyer should be particularly familiar with the applicable rules of appellate procedure in addition to a demonstrated familiarity with the law applicable to the substantive legal issues.

Moreover, a failure to comply with even the most ministerial of format considerations can have a significant impact on the professional credibility of a lawyer. Briefs that fail to comply with format considerations represent a lack of attention to detail and a disregard for the expectations of the appellate court. Indeed, lawyers may be obligated to formally attest to compliance with formatting requirements. Under Federal Rule of Appellate Procedure 32(a)(7)(c), a required certification of compliance filed with an appellate brief is a representation by the lawyer that the brief conforms to certain format requirements. At best, arguments contained in those briefs lose impact. Far worse consequences include fines and admonishments to the lawyer or a dismissal of the appeal, as noted in the cautionary tale below.

Cautionary Tale

Consequences of Failure to Adhere to Format Requirements

A lawyer who disregards format requirements risks dismissal of the appeal. For example, in *Siosen v. Knights of Columbus*,[24] the court dismissed an appeal because the lawyer failed to adhere to the requirements of Federal Rule of Appellate Procedure 28. The court noted that the rule's requirements are mandatory and the brief's failure to conform amounted to an "invitation [for us] to scour the record, research any legal theory that comes to mind, and serve generally as an advocate for appellant."[25] The court concluded that it was disinclined to overlook the lawyer's failures in preparing the brief and therefore dismissed the appeal.

In addition to filing an appellate brief with the appellate court, attorneys typically prepare a joint appendix. Under Federal Rule of Appellate Procedure 30, the appellant has the primary responsibility to prepare the appendix, which is a document comprised of those portions of the lower court proceedings—including docket entries, pleadings, opinions, orders, and the like—that are deemed most relevant to the appeal. Under the federal rules, the appellee may elect to supplement the appendix, and the parties are specifically "encouraged to agree on the contents of the appendix."[26] Thus, the preparation of this written representation of the most

24. 303 F.3d 458 (2d Cir. 2002).

25. *Id.* at 460 (quoting Ernst Haas Studio, Inc. v. Palm Press, Inc., 164 F.3d 110 (2d Cir. 1999).

26. FED. R. APP. P. 30(b)(1).

---

applicable and persuasive materials from the proceedings below is a form of communication between the parties' lawyers, and between those lawyers and the court. Adhering to the rules regarding content and format is an ethical obligation, and working together to achieve some form of an agreement as to the contents of the appendix, given the explicit encouragement to agree upon such contents, requires both ethical adherence to the rules, as well as professionalism between peers.

In sum, as you prepare an appellate brief or responding briefs, be certain that your communication is timely filed. In addition, follow the local rules governing the particulars of format. Finally, be certain that you have made a reasonable inquiry into the facts and law so as to support the truthfulness of your communication of the facts and law set forth in the brief.

Brief Writing Considerations

- Observe general considerations applicable to written communications.

- Obtain court rules to determine format considerations such as font, margin, word limit, and content requirements.

- Carefully review filing requirements.

- Prepare factual representations, paying attention to advocacy and accuracy considerations.

- Review the brief for tone, paying attention to characterization of criticism of the trial court's ruling and the opposing counsel's arguments.

B. Appeal Conferences

Under the federal appellate rules, the court may direct attorneys participating in an appeal to take part in a conference. Appellate attorneys should be familiar with similar rules in their appellate court. An appeal conference may occur before or after oral argument, and is typically intended to "aid in disposing of the proceedings, including simplifying the issues and discussing settlement."[27] The federal rule requires that lawyers, prior to an appeal conference, meet with clients and obtain as much authority as possible in order to facilitate a settlement of the case. Thus, appeal conferences implicate communication between lawyers and opposing counsel, between lawyers and their clients, and between lawyers and the court. You should

---

27. FED. R. APP. P. 33.

be mindful of the obligations of candor when communicating with clients prior to such a conference, noting for the client the objective of the conference with respect to settling the case. You should be mindful of the obligations of truthfulness with respect to representations made to the court and opposing counsel. Further, as with all communication as an advocate, your communications should be guided by professional conventions of civility.

C. Oral Argument

Oral argument represents an opportunity for the appellate lawyer to communicate verbally with the court in an effort to advance her client's position on appeal. As an initial consideration, the appellate lawyer should consider whether to request oral argument for her client. Under Federal Rule of Appellate Procedure 34(a)(1), a party may request oral argument by filing a statement with the court explaining why oral argument should be heard. A lawyer may oppose oral argument in the same manner, by submitting a statement explaining why oral argument need not be permitted. These statements constitute written communications by the lawyer and should conform to all applicable format requirements. Moreover, lawyers should treat these statements as persuasive and prepare them in a manner most likely to achieve the desired effect. Under the federal rules, oral argument will be granted if requested unless three members of a panel of judges unanimously agree that the appeal is frivolous, that the issues have been authoritatively decided, or that the arguments and facts have been adequately advanced in the briefs.[28] Thus, the effective advocate would consult the rule and craft her argument in a manner that corresponds with the noted rationale of the deciding panel.

If oral argument is granted, lawyers for both the appellant and appellee appear before the appellate court to present oral argument and answer questions from the appellate court. The effective, professional advocate understands the purpose of oral argument. The practice of oral argument is not an opportunity for the lawyer to deliver an impressive speech. Further, the term *argument* is a misnomer. If a lawyer is granted the opportunity to appear before the court for oral argument—which is increasingly rare given the crisis of volume at the appellate court level—the objective is to focus the court's attention on the primary arguments and answer any questions the court might have. Justice Ginsberg noted that questions from the bench during oral argument "give counsel a chance to satisfy the court on matters the judges think significant, issues the judges might puzzle over in chambers, and resolve less satisfactorily without counsel's aid."[29]

You are advised, therefore, to focus on preparation for the argument. A professional lawyer should be *absolutely and completely* familiar with the record—members

---

28. FED. R. APP. P. 34(a)(2).

29. The Honorable Ruth Bader Ginsberg, *Remarks on Appellate Advocacy*, 50 S.C. L. REV. 567, 569 (1999).

of the court expect the lawyer to know the facts of his client's case. An effective lawyer should also be familiar with the law. To be effective, you must also know the facts and the rulings of the primary cases relied upon in the brief, as well as those relied upon by the opposing party. In preparing for the argument you should read through the briefs carefully to anticipate the questions the court will ask. Recognize that the argument itself should be carefully planned. Most texts recommend the preparation of "talking points" rather than a full presentation of the argument. Federal Rule of Appellate Procedure 34(c) prohibits a lawyer from reading at length from the brief or other authorities. The court will likely interrupt the argument with questions. A familiarity with the talking points enables a lawyer to resume the argument once questions have been answered.

Once you have prepared your talking points, it is a good idea to plan what you will bring to the courtroom—an outline, note cards, a tabbed document. Consult the rules as to allowable materials. The federal rules require that a lawyer who uses exhibits during oral argument set up the exhibits in the courtroom before the court convenes, and remove them afterward.[30] Whatever you choose to bring, be sure your materials are in a format that allows you to access information easily and quickly. You do not want to waste the court's time looking for materials. The presentation of these materials is a form of nonverbal communication. Adherence to expectations regarding the use of exhibits, both those set forth by rule and by convention, is a manifestation of your professionalism. Thus, your materials at oral argument should be well organized and succinct. You will also feel more prepared for oral argument if you familiarize yourself with the courtroom itself. If possible, attend an oral argument in the courtroom beforehand.

Prepare how you will respond to questions from the bench. An effective attorney will review the briefs and try to anticipate what types of questions the court might ask. Further, prepare yourself to view questions as an opportunity to clarify and reinforce your position. Remember that oral argument should be viewed as a discussion between you and the court, not your opportunity to deliver a lecture. As Justice Ginsberg observed:

> Oral argument, at its best, is an exchange of ideas about the case, a dialogue or discussion between court and counsel. Questions should not be resented as intrusions into a well-planned lecture. To take an example still vivid in my mind, an advocate won no friends at court when he responded to an appellate judge's question: "Forgive me, your honor, but I really don't want to be de-railed onto that trivial point."[31]

---

30. FED. R. APP. P. 34(g).
31. Bader Ginsberg, *supra* note 29, at 569.

In planning for your oral argument questions, familiarize yourself with the court itself. Reading prior decisions of the court and observing arguments before it will enable you to better anticipate your audience and its expectations for oral argument.

Practice Pointers for Oral Argument

Preparation

- Familiarize yourself with the record—know the facts.

- Familiarize yourself with the briefs—know the primary authorities.

- Develop the talking points—keep the arguments simple and focused.

- Plan what you will bring to the courtroom.

- Familiarize yourself with the members of the court and the courtroom.

- Practice your argument.

At the Argument

- Introduce yourself.

- Maintain eye contact with the court.

- Maintain a polite, respectful demeanor.

- Answer the questions asked.

- Avoid distracting gestures.

- Use rebuttal appropriately and effectively.

Be aware not only of the points you hope to make in your dialogue with the court, but also your nonverbal cues. Avoid pacing, finger- or foot-tapping, slouching, and other forms of nonverbal cues that communicate anxiety or impatience. Be absolutely respectful to all members of the court. Do not become impatient with questions and speak slowly and clearly. If you do not understand a question from the bench, attempt to rephrase it, or ask the court to rephrase it. With that said, do not try to recharacterize a question to avoid answering what the court has asked—such evasive techniques will be noted by the court. Try to maintain eye contact with each member of the court. Also, be respectful of the opposing counsel. Nonverbal cues such as eye-rolling, hand gestures, or sighs during the opposing counsel's argument are disrespectful and undermine your own credibility. Finally, on rebuttal stick to the arguments. As with a disparaging tone in an appellate brief, attacks on opposing counsel will be perceived as discourteous and disrespectful. Far from solidifying your position, they will undermine credibility in your otherwise meritorious positions.

Finally, if you represent the appellant, be cognizant of the primary purpose of rebuttal, which is to respond to statements made by opposing counsel. It is not generally good practice to use rebuttal to repeat arguments made previously, or to bring up new ones. Further, if your response is on some minor point, such as an incorrect citation, rebuttal is not appropriate. Do not waste the court's time with such immaterial matters.

D. The Judgment

Once the briefs have been filed and, if applicable, oral argument concluded, the appellate court renders a decision on the appeal. This decision may be accompanied by a written opinion. The lawyer's communicative obligation at this stage is to inform the client of the disposition of the matter and discuss any additional alternatives. As with other forms of communication between lawyer and client, the lawyer is obligated to explain the disposition of the appeal, and any alternative courses of action, to the client in a manner such that the client can make ultimate decisions about how to proceed.

III. POST-APPEAL CONSIDERATIONS

A. Post-Opinion Motions

The party who loses the appeal may file a Motion for Rehearing. Filing deadlines and required content of the motion are likely addressed by local rule and should be conscientiously adhered to. With respect to content, the federal rules note that "[t]he petition must state with particularity each point of law or fact that the petitioner believes the court has overlooked or misapprehended and must argue in support of the petition."[32] The federal rules also do not allow for oral argument or permit the opposing party to respond. A familiarity with the rules of the applicable appellate court is therefore essential, particularly with respect to filing deadlines. A lawyer can be sanctioned for failing to attend to client matters with reasonable promptness. In *In re Cherry*,[33] a lawyer failed to file postconviction relief motions on behalf of his client. The court ruled that the lawyer failed to act with reasonable diligence, citing

---

32. FED. R. APP. P. 40(a)(2).
33. 715 N.E.2d 382 (Ind. 1999).

a comment to the applicable Indiana Rule of Professional Conduct that provided: "a client's interests often can be adversely affected by the passage of time or the change of conditions . . . [e]ven when the client's interests are not affected in substance, however, unreasonable delay can cause a client needless anxiety and undermine confidence in the lawyer's trustworthiness."[34] Moreover, the court concluded that the lawyer failed to make reasonable efforts to expedite litigation and that he had failed to keep his client reasonably informed. Falling below the applicable ethical standards, the lawyer was suspended from the practice of law for sixty days.

B. Petitions for Certiorari

Petitions for certiorari seek to invoke the jurisdiction of a higher or superior court from the ruling of a lower court. The request for a review by a higher court may be referred to as a petition for writ of certiorari or review, or a leave to, or certification for appeal, and is a form of communication between the lawyer and the higher court. The form and substance of such a request is governed by the rules of the applicable jurisdiction. In many instances the party seeking a writ of certiorari from the higher court must first file a notice of intent to apply for the writ of certiorari. This notice is typically directed to the adverse party and may contain references to the opinion being appealed, as well as statements of fact, relief sought, and justification as to why the writ should issue. In addition, the interested party must file the petition for the writ of certiorari, which must include a basis for the granting of the writ. As with all other filings, it is essential that you consult the local procedural rules applicable to seeking review by the higher court.

---

34. *Id.* at 384.

7

TRANSACTIONAL LAWYERING

The term "transactional lawyering" is used here in a broader sense than it may normally be used. Here, it is used not just to define lawyering that is not traditionally litigation-based. It involves pure transactional lawyering such as reviewing and drafting corporate documents, as well as negotiating, reviewing, and drafting contracts. However, as used in this chapter the term also encompasses advising clients about and drafting wills and trusts; advising clients about tax matters and preparing tax-related documents; and advising clients about how to comply with federal, state, and local laws and regulations. In sum, the type of lawyering that falls within this chapter is "planning" lawyering. That is, the primary duty of the lawyer is to make a plan to deal with legal aspects of a particular situation before an adversarial, litigious situation has been created. In such planning, communication is necessarily implicated. Thus, this section addresses the incorporation of ethics and professionalism into your communication as a transactional lawyer. There are some fairly general components of transactional lawyering, some of which are similar or identical to lawyering that occurs during the litigation process. They include

1. *The engagement.* This initial period involves communication between the attorney and the client. It memorializes the business relationship and is usually undertaken by way of a formal written contract.

2. *Communications regarding conflicts.* Many conflicts of interest are apparent at the initial engagement stage and most often should be addressed in the engagement letter. However, because conflicts may arise at other times and because the communication regarding conflicts is so particular, this is dealt with in a separate section of this text.

3. *Research and investigation.* Just as a litigation attorney must investigate the facts of a case and the law applicable to a case, a transactional attorney must investigate the facts of the legal situation that has presented itself and research the applicable law. During this period of research and investigation, the lawyer communicates with the client, with counsel representing other participants, and with other people who may have knowledge that will be helpful in identifying the legal course.

4. *Advising the client.* The attorney advises the client throughout the course of a transaction. Thus, ethics and professionalism relating to communicating advice to a client are dealt with in this section.

5. *Drafting and negotiation.* The attorney must keep in mind various professional, ethical, and legal considerations as he communicates the deal through the drafted document. In addition, after the initial draft is complete, the lawyer is communicating with the client and other participants and their counsel both through the medium of the drafted document as well as through continuing negotiation of the deal.

While this chapter deals first with the engagement and proceeds down the numerated list, like the litigation process, the timing and order of these stages is not precise. This is particularly true because the breadth of "transactional lawyering" as defined in this chapter encompasses such a variety of legal encounters. In addition, when the lawyer is dealing with translating a business deal into legal documents, the process is often recursive. The participants may well have negotiated the primary components of the deal before arriving in the lawyers' offices; however, there is usually ongoing negotiation throughout the drafting process, as well as ongoing advice to the client. Unlike the litigation process, the attorney is unlikely to communicate with court personnel or judges in "transactional lawyering." However, the attorney may, at times, communicate with government employees and officials and other professionals who can assist in crafting and negotiating the deal. Also, while not as evident as in the litigation process, the attorney must continue to adhere in her communications to the rules of ethics, laws and regulations, and conventions of professionalism. Responsibilities with respect to transactional lawyering, like those in litigation legal practice, implicate the general considerations in ethical and professional communication discussed in Chapter 2.

I. THE ENGAGEMENT

A. The Engagement Communicates Competence

As noted in Chapter 4 dealing with pretrial advocacy, in accepting representation, the lawyer communicates to the client that she is competent to handle the transactional matter at hand. Not only does Model Rule of Professional Conduct 1.1 require competence, it defines it as the "legal knowledge, skill, thoroughness and preparation reasonably necessary for the representation." While such competence can be acquired through self-education, it is particularly important to consider the limitations of self-education in the context of complex transactional representations. In any event, the attorney must be aware that in accepting the representation, she is communicating that she is competent through experience, self-education, or association with another attorney to carry out the legal duties of the transaction at hand.

B. Organizational Clients and Clients with Diminished Capacity

Often in a transactional setting, the first question is with whom the attorney should communicate when the client is an organizational client. As noted in Chapter 2, dealing with general considerations of communicating in representation, Model Rule of Professional Conduct 1.13 provides guidance in this matter. Because this is likely to arise frequently in the transactional setting, those considerations outlined in Chapter 2 must be taken into consideration in communicating with the organizational client.

In addition to organizational clients, there is some question about appropriate persons with whom to communicate when the client has a diminished capacity. Again, this topic is addressed in greater detail in Chapter 2, and the attorney should refer to that chapter to guide her communications with the diminished capacity client.

C. Client Engagement Letter

Once the attorney determines that the circumstances will allow her to represent the client, she may enter into an attorney-client relationship. In addition to the general considerations noted in Chapter 2 with respect to written communications and letters and in Chapter 3 with respect to conflicts of interest, there are certain considerations specific to client engagement letters. A client engagement letter is a letter written to the client in which the lawyer sets out the parameters of the attorney-client relationship. While not always required by the ethical rules, you should always define the attorney-client relationship in formal letter format.

Model Rule of Professional Conduct 1.5 prohibits unreasonable fees and provides a number of considerations to determine the reasonableness of the attorney's fees. While the reasonableness of the fee is beyond the scope of this text, additional provisions in that rule deal with communication with respect to attorney fees. Model Rule of Professional Conduct 1.5(b) provides:

> The scope of the representation and the basis or rate of the fee and expenses for which the client will be responsible shall be communicated to the client, preferably in writing, before or within a reasonable time after commencing the representation, except when the lawyer will charge a regularly represented client on the same basis or rate. Any changes in the basis or rate of the fee or expenses shall also be communicated to the client.

While a written statement about fees and the nature of the relationship is not required by the rules, comment 2 notes that "[a] written statement concerning the terms of the engagement reduces the possibility of misunderstanding."[1] Thus, while

---

1. MODEL RULES OF PROF'L CONDUCT R. 1.2 cmt. 2 (2008).

not required, you are advised to provide a written letter regarding the nature of the relationship and fees.

The engagement letter should identify the scope of the representation with specificity. Usually the identification of a client matter in a letter of engagement indicates that the attorney will represent the client in all aspects of that client matter. However, in some instances, the scope of representation may be limited. Model Rule of Professional Conduct 1.2(c) provides that "[a] lawyer may limit the scope of the representation if the limitation is reasonable under the circumstances and the client gives informed consent." There are various reasons for limiting the representation. A client may want to limit the representation to initial advice and then make a determination whether to extend the representation. As noted by the rule, however, the limitation on representation must be reasonable. As noted in comment 7, if the lawyer and client attempt to limit representation to a brief telephone consultation, but such limitation would likely be unreasonable to yield competent advice, such a limitation would not be in line with the rule.[2] In sum, the scope of representation must be defined and a limited representation must be specifically identified and outlined.

The engagement letter should include the legal fees that will be charged, including how those charges will be computed. Therefore, if the fees will be charged at an hourly rate for services, you should indicate for whom such charges will be incurred, the specific rates for each person who performs on behalf of the client, and the types of services that are included (e.g., preparation, research, travel, interoffice memos, correspondence, etc.). Further, if fees are charged on an hourly basis, the increments in which the hour is divided should be made known to the client. The letter should specifically identify other costs and expenses for which the client will be responsible. Examples include long distance telephone charges, messenger or delivery fees, postage expenses, in-office photocopying and its rate, parking, mileage, investigation expenses, and expenses of consultants employed on behalf of the client. All of these specifics help establish the terms of the representation and, therefore, reinforce conventions of professionalism.

The engagement letter should indicate when the client should expect statements from the firm and when payment of outstanding fees and expenses is expected. If you receive a retainer, you should carefully outline the mechanism by which you expect to draw client funds from the retainer. The engagement letter should also provide a place where the client signs the letter and acknowledges and agrees to its contents.

In addition to these rules, the Statute of Frauds applicable in most states requires any agreement that is not to be completed within one year to be in writing and signed by the party to be charged. In sum, it is advisable to have all letters of

---

2. *Id.* cmt. 7.

engagement in writing and signed by the client. If the Statute of Frauds is applicable, the engagement letter must be in writing.

Finally, the attorney must be aware of the potential for conflicts of interest, and, if evident at the time of the engagement letter, the lawyer should incorporate the required communication about client conflicts into the engagement letter.

All Client Engagement Letters Should

- Be directed to the client and, in the case of organizational entities, to the appropriate constituents of the client.

- Be in writing.

- Be signed by the client.

- Identify the scope of representation.

- Identify limitations on representation and obtain informed consent where necessary.

- State what the fee will be (flat fee or hourly fee).

- Identify how the fee will be computed.

- Identify the services for which a fee will be charged.

- Identify expenses that will be charged to the client.

- Notify the client how often the client will be billed.

- Communicate when the attorney will expect payment for the amounts billed.

- If a retainer is used, explain the mechanism by which the attorney will use the retainer.

- Advise of concurrent conflicts if necessary.

II. COMMUNICATIONS REGARDING CONFLICTS

Conflicts of interest may arise in transactional lawyering, and ethical rules require the lawyer to follow a very specific protocol for communicating regarding these conflicts. Communication regarding conflicts of interest is dealt with in detail in Chapter 3, and the attorney should refer to that chapter when confronted with conflicts. Suffice it to say here, in addition to the ethical rules pertaining to conflicts

---

and the issues of communication encompassing conflicts, notions of professionalism require the attorney to communicate and attend to conflicts with the client. A transactional attorney hopes to continue representation of her clients for a lengthy period of time. Honestly dealing with and communicating conflicts when they arise will promote a trusting relationship with the client and encourage the longevity of the relationship beyond the current legal matter.

III. RESEARCH AND INVESTIGATION

As in litigation lawyering, the transactional attorney must both research the law and investigate the facts. In the case of a matter that will be litigated, during an informal investigation period the attorney conducts an inquiry to determine whether the facts and law support the filing of a lawsuit. In the context of transactional lawyering, the attorney similarly investigates the facts to determine what the transaction is intended to be and the context within which it will occur. In addition, the lawyer must investigate the law to determine how to translate the intent of the client and other participants into a legal document. As in litigation representation, there are two components to this process: investigation of the law and investigation of the facts. As noted in prior chapters, while investigation of the law is essential to the process of determining how to create a legally effective document, the investigation process itself does not implicate notions of professionalism related to communication. Therefore, this portion of the text will concentrate on an attorney's investigation of the facts and her communicative behavior in the context of fact-gathering.

In the litigation setting, there are two phases within which facts are discovered. One is the informal investigation period that occurs before a lawsuit is filed; the other is the formal investigation discovery process. In transactional lawyering, there is no court-enforced discovery process. In addition, while the persons involved in a given transaction do not want to reveal all of the facts known to them, the sharing of factual information is generally advantageous to all parties and, therefore, much less adversarial than in the litigation setting. So, while there is no court-enforced mechanism by which to discover facts, the parties are motivated to share facts with one another in order to "seal the deal." Investigation of the facts includes obtaining facts by interviewing clients and other persons and obtaining factual information by e-mail and letter. In transactional lawyering, the lawyer is more focused on communicating facts to the participants, both verbally and in writing.

Because you will communicate both verbally and in writing with others to develop the facts, you must be mindful of those general considerations related to both oral and written communications outlined in Chapter 2. In addition, during this process, with respect to both written and oral communications, the lawyer must be mindful of ethical rules requiring an attorney to be truthful, limiting communication with represented parties, limiting communication with unrepresented persons, and limiting the use of obtaining information by methods that infringe upon the rights of others.

A. Communications Must Be Truthful

In developing the facts that support the transaction at hand, one of the ethical considerations related to communications is the requirement the lawyer make truthful statements to others. Model Rule of Professional Conduct 4.1 prohibits a lawyer from making "a false statement of material fact or law to a third person." The rule also prohibits the lawyer from failing "to disclose a material fact when disclosure is necessary to avoid assisting a criminal or fraudulent act by a client" unless disclosure is prohibited by Model Rule of Professional Conduct 1.6, which requires the lawyer to preserve the client's confidences.

Clearly, this rule prohibits a direct misrepresentation. Also, comment 1 prohibits an attorney from affirming a statement of another person when the attorney knows that statement to be false.[3] When you are seeking to obtain information from others, conventions of professionalism also require you to identify yourself as an attorney and identify your client. You should be mindful of preserving the client's confidences, but in the transactional setting you may be motivated to share relevant factual information as well. Nevertheless, you are encouraged to keep in mind that, because of the element of negotiation present in transactional lawyering, not all factual statements are considered to be statements of material fact. Some statements while seemingly factual in nature are not considered to be material facts in the context of negotiation because there is some component of either opinion, assessment, or negotiability attached to them. For example, comment 2 notes that "[e]stimates of price or value placed on the subject of a transaction" are not generally considered to be material statements of fact within the meaning of this rule.[4] Estimates of price and value may vary according to the lawyer's particular assessment or opinion and, therefore, are not "statements of material fact."

B. Communications with Represented Persons

As in the case of litigation, communication with persons represented by counsel is prohibited by Model Rule of Professional Conduct 4.2 unless the attorney has obtained the consent of the other attorney, is authorized to speak with the person by law, or has obtained a court order to speak with that person. Thus, when conducting a factual inquiry, you are prohibited from communicating about the matter at hand with individuals who are represented by counsel. This is true regardless of whether that person's interests directly oppose your client's or not. Comment 3 also makes clear that communication with a represented individual is prohibited "even though

---

3. MODEL RULES OF PROF'L CONDUCT R. 4.1 cmt. 1 (2008).

4. *Id.* cmt. 2.

the represented person initiates or consents to the communication."[5] If the person initiates the communication, it is incumbent upon the attorney to immediately end the communication. Notably, the rule prohibits communication with a represented person only with respect to the legal matter at issue. Thus, you may very well communicate with persons about other matters unrelated to the legal matter at issue.[6]

In the transactional setting, it is important to understand that when an organization is represented, Model Rule of Professional Conduct 4.2 also "prohibits communications with a constituent of the organization who supervises, directs or regularly consults with the organization's lawyer concerning the matter or has authority to obligate the organization with respect to the matter or whose act or omission in connection with the matter may be imputed to the organization for purposes of civil or criminal liability."[7] On the other hand, a lawyer may communicate directly with a former constituent of the organization.[8]

C. Communications with Unrepresented Persons

Model Rule of Professional Conduct 4.3 applies to an attorney's communications with unrepresented parties. Thus, when the lawyer communicates with unrepresented persons in her pursuit of obtaining information in the transactional setting, she must "not state or imply that the lawyer is disinterested." Rule 4.3 not only prohibits an affirmative statement or implication that the lawyer is disinterested, but also requires that "[w]hen the lawyer knows or reasonably should know that the unrepresented person misunderstands the lawyer's role in the matter, the lawyer shall make reasonable efforts to correct the misunderstanding." That is, the lawyer has an affirmative duty to correct the misunderstanding of the person. As indicated by comment 1, such misunderstandings can be clarified by "identify[ing] the lawyer's client and, where necessary, explain[ing] that the client has interests opposed to those of the unrepresented person."[9] In the context of transactional lawyering, this situation may arise during the process of obtaining information about a business or corporation on the other side of the transaction. Whether the attorney is conducting a due diligence investigation or otherwise trying to acquire such information, the attorney must clearly reveal her representation to the representative of the business or corporation from whom she is seeking information.

As noted in Chapter 3 dealing with conflicts, Model Rule of Professional Conduct 1.13 addresses an attorney's obligations with respect to communicating with unrepresented constituents of the organization that the attorney represents. In the process of fact-gathering, a transactional attorney may have occasion to

---

5. *Id.* 4.2 cmt. 3.
6. *Id.* cmt. 4.
7. *Id.* cmt. 7.
8. *Id.*
9. *Id.* 4.3 cmt. 1.

communicate with shareholders, employees, or other constituents of both the organization she represents and the shareholders, employees, or other constituents of other organizations participating in the business transaction. To the extent that there is no conflict between the unrepresented constituents and the client, the attorney need only reveal the representation. However, if a conflict between the unrepresented constituents and the organization is revealed in the process of fact-gathering, the attorney should deal with such conflicts of interest as outlined more fully in Chapter 3.

Model Rule of Professional Conduct 4.3 also contains a specific prohibition that the lawyers not give legal advice to unrepresented persons if those persons "are or have a reasonable possibility of being in conflict with the interests of the client." Thus, when seeking to obtain information by communicating with unrepresented persons who may have interests adverse to the client, be careful to avoid the appearance of rendering legal advice to such persons. In the case of transactional lawyering, you must be careful not to create the appearance of representing both the client and the other unrepresented participants.

D. Communications Regarding Inadvertently Received Documents

Model Rule of Professional Conduct 4.4(b) relates specifically to documentary information. It provides that "[a] lawyer who receives a document relating to the representation of the lawyer's client and knows or reasonably should know that the

---

A Lawyer Who Is Gathering Information

1. Must be truthful.

2. May not, without authority from opposing counsel, communicate directly with another participant to the transaction who is represented or with that participant's constituents.

3. Must inform constituents of an organization whose interests are adverse to the organization that the attorney represents the organization and does not represent the constituents.

4. May not give legal advice to unrepresented persons if those persons have a conflicting or potentially conflicting interest.

5. Must notify the sender when the attorney receives a document that she should not have received.

---

document was inadvertently sent shall promptly notify the sender." This rule is intended to deal with a situation where an attorney mistakenly receives a document from an adverse person or attorney, which could occur during the investigative stage of transactional representation. In fact, because a great deal of written documentation passes between transactional attorneys in facilitating a business deal, the possibility of inadvertent receipt of documents is more likely in the transactional setting. Rule 4.4(b) imposes a duty on the lawyer to communicate with the sender that the lawyer has received the document. Comment 2 to the rule specifically notes that the word "document" includes electronic methods of communication (including e-mail) "subject to being read or put into readable format."[10]

IV. ADVISING THE CLIENT

In the chapter on Pretrial Advocacy, this text focused considerably on the initial advice letter because an initial advice letter is fairly standard in the course of representing clients in the context of litigation. In the context of transactional lawyering, there may sometimes be an identifiable initial advice letter to the client, which may be particularly true in the case of estate planning, tax advice, and the like. However, throughout the course of negotiating and translating the desires of the client into a legally effective document, the lawyer will advise the client in a variety of ways. In some instances, the client comes to the attorney having negotiated the major components of the deal. The role of the lawyer in that instance is to advise the client of additional components that the client might consider, as well as the legal and other implications of all of the components of the deal (both those negotiated by the client and by the lawyer). Thus, this section focuses on the professional ethical considerations of advising the client, keeping in mind that at times an initial advice letter may be a viable method of delivering that communication.

A. Duty to Communicate Candidly and Fully

Model Rule of Professional Conduct 2.1, which addresses the lawyer's role as advisor, provides:

> In representing a client, a lawyer shall exercise independent professional judgment and render candid advice. In rendering candid advice, a lawyer may refer not only to the law but to other considerations such as moral, economic, social and political factors, that may be relevant to the client's situation.

Comment 1 to Rule 2.1 makes clear that the duty of providing the client with straightforward, honest advice should not be tempered by a lawyer's hesitancy to present unfavorable information. While it is often uncomfortable to honestly

---

10. *Id.* 4.4 cmt. 2

approach unfavorable or unpleasant facts and options, the lawyer has an affirmative, ethical obligation to do so.

Not only does the lawyer have a duty of candor, but he also has a duty to advise the client as to considerations beyond the scope of the law. As noted by comment 2, purely technical legal advice is not always sufficient, particularly "where practical considerations, such as cost or effects on other people, are predominant."[11] Thus, while the legal implications of a particular transactional matter may be fairly straightforward, the practical implications may give rise to additional discussions between you and your client. The extent to which a lawyer must advise a client as to other considerations may be impacted by the sophistication of the client. A more sophisticated client may understand the limitations of receiving purely legal advice. Indeed, some clients may prefer it. However, you must evaluate whether solely giving legal advice will fulfill the lawyer's duty to advise, and that evaluation must take into account the nature of the client.

The duty to advise a client on nonlegal considerations may also require the attorney to direct the client to consult with professionals in other fields who may give the client the type of nonlegal direction needed in a particular situation. In the transactional setting, "business matters can involve problems within the competence of the accounting profession or of financial specialists."[12] If the requirement of competence requires it, the lawyer should recommend a professional in another field.

In any event, in the context of transactional drafting, the lawyer will often be called upon to advise the client beyond the negotiated terms that the client brings to the lawyer. Often clients have negotiated the major components of a deal. However, the lawyer's duty to advise on legal and nonlegal matters requires the lawyer to bring to the client's attention other issues that might arise in the course of dealings between the parties. For example, in the negotiation of an employment agreement, if the parties have failed to negotiate a covenant not to compete, the lawyer must advise whether such a provision would be beneficial. In the sale of a business agreement, the client may not have negotiated what will happen to certain property of the business between time of the sales agreement and the closing, and yet such a matter is of importance to both parties. The attorney has a duty to anticipate how the transaction may play out and prevent unfavorable consequences.

While comment 5 to Rule 2.1 indicates that generally "a lawyer is not expected to give advice until asked by the client," that comment also provides that

> when a lawyer knows that a client proposes a course of action that
> is likely to result in substantial adverse legal consequences to the
> client, the lawyer's duty to the client under Rule 1.4 may require

---

11. *Id.* 2.1 cmt. 2.
12. *Id.* cmt. 4.

that the lawyer offer advice if the client's course of action is related to the representation.[13]

Further, because Model Rule of Professional Conduct 1.4 imposes a duty upon the lawyer to keep the client informed about the matter related to client representation, there may be instances where the attorney may offer unsolicited advice related to the matter. As noted above, in the transactional setting, the attorney's unsolicited advice is often tacitly expected.

The lawyer also has a responsibility to advise the client of the potential alternative actions. In advising as to alternative actions, the lawyer must pay particular attention to the division of authority between the lawyer and client as outlined by Model Rule of Professional Conduct 1.2. Generally, that rule requires the lawyer to "abide by a client's decisions concerning the objectives of representation." Model Rule of Professional Conduct 1.4 requires the lawyer to "reasonably consult with the client about the means by which the client's objectives are to be accomplished." In the context of transactional lawyering, the role of the lawyer is to translate the wishes of the client into legally effective documents. In practical terms, this means that the attorney must outline the alternatives available to the client, both legal action and otherwise. In addition, to allow the client to make an informed decision, the benefits and costs of each alternative action should be outlined. The attorney may advise the client as to the course of action that the attorney views to be the best; however, she should be clear in conveying to the client that the ultimate authority rests with the client.

B. Duty to Provide Consultative and Explanatory Communications

Under Model Rule of Professional Conduct 1.4, a lawyer has an obligation to both consult with the client about how the objectives of representation will be accomplished and to provide the client with explanations regarding representation. With respect to transactional lawyering, there is likely more consultative communication that will be exchanged between attorney and client than in the litigation setting. It is generally the client who has more intimate knowledge of the elements of a transaction and the real world goals that the parties seek to obtain. Thus, consultation with the client begins at the start of the representation and continues throughout as the attorney and client exchange ideas about how to best achieve the client's objectives. Two considerations should be kept in mind in determining whether the attorney must consult with the client and the method by which the client must be consulted: the feasibility of communicating and the importance of the decision.

Comment 3 notes that "feasibility" of communication is an important consideration in determining whether communication is required at all. Thus, in some situations, such as "during a trial when an immediate decision must be made," the

---

13. *Id.* cmt. 5.

exigency of the situation will make it such that consultative communication is not feasible.[14] In most instances of transactional representation, such exigencies will not exist. Most transactional representations occur over a period of time and under non-emergency circumstances. However, situations such as abrupt changes in the market or competitive constraints may sometimes create a situation in which an attorney must act on the known desires of her client without consultation.

Assuming that feasibility will rarely be a barrier to communication in transactional representation, the second consideration in determining whether a consultative communication is necessary is the importance of the decision, or whether there is a legitimate need for the client's participation in the decision-making process. Thus, ministerial decisions, such as whether to send a letter by regular mail or courier, while related to the client's objectives with regard to representation, would not generally be deemed a matter of sufficient importance to the client to require consultation. On the other hand, the timing of payments to be included in a contract is clearly an important matter about which the client might expect to be, and likely should be, consulted.

In the litigation setting, where consultation is required, such communication is generally accomplished by formal letter. In the transactional setting, particularly in the course of negotiating and drafting, the lawyer may communicate with the client less formally and more often by e-mail and telephone. At some point, however, as the deal nears completion, the lawyer should memorialize in a letter the essential terms of the transaction and the decisions that have been made by the client in the course of consultation. To evidence the consultation and consent of the client, it is best to obtain written authorization from the client or send the client a letter confirming that the consultation occurred, that the client was advised, and that the client chose a particular method of satisfying the client's objectives.

Related to the duty to reasonably consult with the client is the lawyer's duty, as identified in Model Rule of Professional Conduct 1.4(b), to "explain a matter to the extent reasonably necessary to permit the client to make informed decisions regarding the representation." This rule governs how much information must be explained to the client in order for the client to genuinely participate in the means by which the client's objectives are achieved. "The client should have sufficient information to participate intelligently in decisions concerning the objectives of the representation and the means by which they are to be pursued, to the extent the client is willing and able to do so."[15] The sufficiency of information is related to the complexity of the client matter and the complexity of the particular course of action under consideration, as well as the sophistication of the client. Sufficiency of information will necessarily depend on the circumstances and be determined on a case-by-case basis. Thus, comment 5 notes that a lawyer should almost always review with her client

---

14. MODEL RULES OF PROF'L CONDUCT R. 1.4 cmt. 3 (2008).

15. *Id.* cmt. 5.

all important provisions in a negotiation proposal before agreeing to the proposal.[16] On the other hand, discussing all aspects of your strategy for negotiation is not necessary to allow the client's intelligent participation in decision-making.

C. Duty to Provide Informative Communication

Not only does a lawyer have a duty to consult with the client and explain matters to the client in order for the client to make informed decisions, Model Rule of Professional Conduct 1.4(a)(3) also requires that the attorney "keep the client reasonably informed about the status of the matter." As noted in comment 4, "[a] lawyer's regular communication with clients will minimize the occasions on which a client will need to request information concerning the representation."[17] As a practical matter, clients are frustrated by the inability to contact their lawyers, as well as their lawyer's failure to communicate with them on a regular basis. A lawyer should calendar each file to ensure that she communicates with clients on an on-going basis. Even when there has been no activity in the case the lawyer should communicate with the client at least as often as the client receives a bill from the lawyer. If there has been no activity, the lawyer should communicate that information and the reason for the inactivity to the client. Activity on the file should be communicated at the earliest possible time. Even when engaging in legal research, the client should be notified of that activity. While each lawyer has hundreds of files, most clients have only one or two lawsuits going, and each client wants the assurance that his legal matter is receiving the attention he believes it deserves.

The duty to keep the client informed may be fulfilled either by telephone communications, e-mail communications, or formal letters. As noted above, in the transactional lawyering context, when a transaction is in the process of being negotiated, drafted, and translated into a legal document, there is likely to be more telephone and e-mail communication with the client. Remember, however, that if the client has received a series of updates by e-mail or telephone, periodically a formal letter summarizing the status of the case is recommended. If the update is of considerable importance or length, a formal letter is the recommended method of communicating.

In addition to requiring the lawyer to keep the client informed about the case, Model Rule of Professional Conduct 1.4(a)(4) requires the lawyer to "promptly comply with reasonable requests for information." As noted by comment 4, while the rule requires a prompt response to reasonable requests "if a prompt response is not feasible, [the rule requires] that the lawyer, or a member of the lawyer's staff, acknowledge receipt of the request and advise the client when a response may be expected."[18] Interestingly, this rule is tempered by comment 7, which acknowledges

---

16. *Id.*

17. *Id.* 1.4 cmt. 4.

18. *Id.*

that in some situations "a lawyer may be justified in delaying transmission of information when the client would be likely to react imprudently to an immediate communication."[19] Further, an attorney may withhold information when required to do so by court orders or rules.[20] Nevertheless, withholding of information is not allowed merely because it is convenient or advantageous to the lawyer or some other person.

In addition, comment 4 directs that "[c]lient telephone calls should be promptly returned or acknowledged."[21] Application of this rule is straightforward; the attorney should promptly respond to or acknowledge requests for information and any telephone communications. While not specifically addressed by the rule or comments, the attorney should also promptly respond or acknowledge e-mail communications. A good rule of thumb is to respond to telephone and e-mail communications from clients within twenty-four hours.

D. Duty to Refrain from Advising Clients to Engage in Criminal/Fraudulent Conduct

Model Rule of Professional Conduct 1.2(d) further provides:

> A lawyer shall not counsel a client to engage, or assist a client, in conduct that the lawyer knows is criminal or fraudulent, but a lawyer may discuss the legal consequence of any proposed course of conduct with a client and may counsel or assist a client to make a good faith effort to determine the validity, scope, meaning or application of the law.

What this means is that your advice should never present criminal or fraudulent conduct as viable alternatives. In the context of transactional lawyering, however, a lawyer is not prohibited from advising her client as to alternatives that will expose the client to nonfraudulent civil liability. While allowing or counseling a client to choose to commit a crime or fraud is clearly prohibited, a client may choose to expose himself to nonfraudulent civil liability.

In addition, comment 9 notes that the provision precluding a lawyer from encouraging or assisting a client in criminal or fraudulent conduct "does not preclude a lawyer from giving an honest opinion about the actual consequences that appear likely to result from a client's conduct."[22] Thus, it appears that a lawyer may advise a client that existing conduct may constitute a crime or fraud and advise as to the repercussions of such conduct. Likewise, it appears that a lawyer may advise that a

---

19. *Id.* cmt. 7.
20. *Id.*
21. *Id.* cmt. 4.
22. *Id.* 1.2 cmt. 9.

client is legally prohibited from a particular alternative because it involves criminal or fraudulent conduct. Additionally, comment 13 cautions that "[i]f a lawyer comes to know or reasonably should know that a client expects assistance not permitted by the Rules of Professional Conduct or other law" the lawyer must follow Rule 1.4(a)(5), requiring the lawyer to notify the client that the lawyer will not be able to proceed with the requested action or assistance.[23]

E. Duty to Communicate with Clients of Conflicts and Disclosures

As noted in Chapter 3, there are many instances where the attorney must advise the client of a variety of conflicts and obtain informed consent to the continued representation. Often those conflicts present themselves at the outset of the representation. However, to the extent that such conflicts arise later, the required communications with the client about those conflicts as set forth in Chapter 3 should be followed. In addition, under Model Rule of Professional Conduct 1.6(a), the attorney may not disclose confidential information of the client unless the attorney has obtained informed consent to such disclosure. Thus, it is possible that a client may consent to the disclosure of confidential information in the negotiation of a business deal. In such instances, the attorney's communication with the client in which he advises the client of the need for informed consent should include "a disclosure of facts and circumstances giving rise to the situation, any explanation reasonably necessary to inform the client or the person of the material advantages and disadvantages of the proposed course of conflict and a discussion of the client's or other person's options and alternatives."[24] While not required by the rule, it is advisable to provide this information in writing to the client and obtain the client's signed consent to the disclosure.

F. Duty to Communicate Potential Constituent Wrongdoing

Pursuant to Model Rule of Professional Conduct 1.13(b), when a lawyer representing an organization becomes aware that "the organization is likely to be substantially injured by action of an officer or other constituent that violates a legal obligation to the organization or is in violation of law that might be imputed to the organization, the lawyer must proceed as is reasonably necessary in the best interest of the organization."[25] At times, this will require communication of the matter to a higher authority in the organization. To determine whether such communication is required, comment 4 indicates that the lawyer must evaluate (1) the seriousness of the violation, (2) the consequences of the violation, (3) the organizational responsibility of the person involved, (4) the organizational policies related to the matter, and (5) any other relevant information. Comment 4 notes that generally referral to

23. *Id.* 1.2 cmt. 13.
24. *Id.* 1.0 cmt. 6.
25. MODEL RULES OF PROF'L CONDUCT R. 1.13 cmt. 3 (2008).

a higher authority within the organization is necessary, however, there may be situations where referral is not necessary and the lawyer may request the constituent to reconsider the action.[26] This most likely would be appropriate when the constituent's action was grounded in innocent motivation.

Advising Clients

1. The lawyer must communicate fully and candidly with the client.

2. The lawyer must consult with the client about how the client objectives will be achieved.

3. The lawyer must explain matters sufficiently so that the client can make informed decisions.

4. The lawyer must keep the client updated on the status of the client matter.

5. The lawyer must communicate regarding conflicts or disclosures of client information.

6. The lawyer must communicate wrongdoing by constituents.

7. The lawyer must promptly respond to requests for information, telephone calls, and e-mails.

8. The lawyer must refrain from advising clients to engage in criminal or fraudulent conduct.

9. When the client appears to want improper or illegal assistance, the lawyer must communicate the limitations of the representation.

G. Duty to Communicate about Lawyer Limitations

Rule 1.4(a)(5) requires the attorney to "consult with the client about any relevant limitation on the lawyer's conduct when the lawyer knows that the client expects assistance not permitted by the rules of Professional Conduct or other law." As noted above, in providing advice to a client, an attorney may not counsel the client to engage in fraud or other criminal conduct. This rule expands on that notion by requiring the attorney to advise the client that the attorney is unable to provide assistance if the assistance expected by the client is impermissible under the rules. Because of the delicate nature of this consultation, it is suggested that the

---

26. *Id.* cmt. 4.

communication of the attorney's limitations be in writing and specifically outline those rules or laws that prohibit the expected behavior.

V. DRAFTING AND NEGOTIATING

In addressing the ethical and professional requirements of communicating in the context of transactional lawyering, it is difficult to parse out the stages of drafting and negotiating. To a certain extent, many of the essential elements of a transaction are discussed during a negotiation period before drafting begins (and sometimes before lawyers even become involved in the process). While the "drafting" of a transactional document may involve actual drafting by the "drafting attorney," it may also involve reviewing, commenting, and editing by an attorney for another party to the transaction. To the extent that a "drafted" document goes through revisions during this process of drafting, reviewing, and commenting, the negotiation of the deal continues. Thus, the considerations noted under this section are recurrent during this phase of drafting, negotiating, reviewing, and commenting.

A. Communicate to Client Desirability of Being the Drafting Attorney

An attorney who represents a party in a transactional matter may yield the role of drafting to another party's attorney. However, the ability to act as the primary drafting attorney is generally so advantageous that your client should be apprised of the advantages. As noted earlier, Model Rule of Professional Conduct 2.1 provides:

> In rendering advice, a lawyer may refer not only to the law, but to other considerations such as moral, economic, social and political factors, that may be relevant to the client's situation.

Advising your client of the advantage of acting as the drafting attorney falls within this rule. The attorney who firsts drafts the transaction has the advantage of crafting the structure and all of the provisions of the contract in a manner favorable to the client. While the document may undergo substantial revision and editing, the attorney has the ability to include all considerations relevant to the client in the first draft; thus, rather than bargaining for change during revision, the drafting attorney is merely bargaining to maintain the already drafted document.

Nonetheless, to have counsel acting as drafting attorney often is more expensive for the client. Clearly, it is more time-consuming to draft an original document than to comment and seek revision of an already drafted document. Thus, you must also apprise the client of the financial disadvantage often entailed in acting as the drafting attorney.

B. Communicate the Deal in the Most Legally Effective Manner

Transactional lawyering ultimately produces a document that has a legal effect. Transactional documents do not communicate an analysis or argument about how the law will be applied to a particular situation; rather, they communicate a legal transaction. Thus, to the extent that the lawyer is called upon by Model Rule of Professional Conduct 1.1 to "provide competent representation to a client," the lawyer must be able to competently communicate the transaction through a legally effective document. As noted by Rule 1.1, "[c]ompetent representation requires the legal knowledge, skill, thoroughness and preparation reasonably necessary for the representation." That rule provides for acquiring competence through self-education or association with another lawyer. The difficulty, as it relates to drafting documents, is that most attorneys assume by reason of their law degree and bar passage that they are competent to draft legally effective documents without ever having had any training in the mechanics of transactional drafting. If the attorney has not taken such a course in law school, it is incumbent upon the attorney to educate herself in those mechanics before embarking upon drafting documents. It is likely that without such training, the lawyer will often fail to communicate the deal, as negotiated by client and lawyer, into a legally effective document.

Cautionary Tale

A Burrito Is Not a Sandwich[27]

The importance of being able to competently communicate the client's deal is aptly illustrated by a lawsuit in which Panera Bread sued a shopping center claiming that the shopping center had violated a lease agreement that restricted the mall from renting to another "sandwich" shop. Panera Bread claimed breach of contract when the shopping center signed a lease with Qdoba, a restaurant selling burritos, tacos, and quesadillas. Panera Bread argued that the burritos sold by Qdoba were within the meaning of "sandwich," and both sides called high-profile experts in the restaurant and food industry to testify as to definition of "sandwich." Based on the testimony, the court ruled that a burrito is not a sandwich because "a sandwich is not commonly understood to include burritos, tacos, and quesadillas, which are typically made with a single tortilla . . . ." The lawyers for Panera Bread could easily have avoided the lawsuit if they had defined "sandwich" in the definitions section of the contract.

---

27. White City Shopping Ctr., LP v. PR Rest., LLC, 21 Mass. L. Rep. 565 (Mass. 2006)

C. Communications with Opposing Counsel and Other Parties

In the course of negotiation, drafting, review, and editing, the attorney will often have the occasion to discuss the terms of the transaction with other persons, parties, and counsel. The question then arises as to the extent to which the attorney must inform these participants of the terms of the deal, the changes made in a draft of a contract, and the like. In some instances, the identity of the party will affect the extent to which the attorney must communicate information to other participants.

1. Generally Negotiation Communications Must Be Truthful

Under Model Rule of Professional Conduct 4.1, an attorney is prohibited from knowingly "making a false statement of a material fact to a third person," as well as failing "to disclose a material fact when disclosure is necessary to avoid assisting a criminal or fraudulent act by a client." Further, under Model Rule of Professional Conduct 8.4, it is deemed to be professional misconduct not only when the attorney engages in fraud, deceit, or misrepresentation, but also when the attorney engages in "dishonesty." For the transactional attorney, the difficult issue in the course of negotiations is determining what constitutes a "material fact" and "dishonesty."

Comment 2 to Rule 4.1 gives some insight into these issues—conventions of negotiation recognize that certain types of information discussed in the course of negotiations are not generally understood to be "statements of material fact." For example, "[e]stimates of price or value placed on the subject of a transaction and a party's intentions as to an acceptable settlement of a claim," as well as "the existence of an undisclosed principal except where nondisclosure of the principal would constitute fraud" are generally not considered statements of material fact.[28]

There is some inconsistency in the profession as to what characterizations of fact are acceptable in the course of negotiations and what characterizations are not acceptable. However, it is likely that an attorney need not disclose information such as the client's bottom line on negotiated matters. Additionally, where the parties have the opportunity to evaluate the value of the subject of the contract, the attorney need not provide his client's opinion as to that value. The questions that ought to be asked in determining whether the information must be disclosed are (1) whether there is sufficient factual information available to both sides to objectively evaluate the terms of the deal; and (2) whether the information is a negotiable "position" of the client, rather than an objective fact.

2. Communications with Counsel

Because an attorney has a duty to disclose material facts, there may be times in the course of negotiations when an attorney must advise even opposing counsel of the presence or absence of terms in the drafted document as well as changes that

---

28. MODEL RULES OF PROF'L CONDUCT R. 1.1 cmt. 2 (2008).

have been made in the drafted document. A key to that communication is the extent to which a provision is omitted, added, or changed when that provision has been the subject of negotiation, either written or oral, between the parties.

The process of exchanging drafts is part of the process of negotiating the terms of the agreement. During drafting and exchanging drafts, the first question to arise is to what extent one attorney must make the opposing attorney aware of unfavorable terms in the original draft. While the drafting attorney must draft the document that has been negotiated, the drafting attorney need not make opposing counsel aware of unfavorable terms in the original draft if those terms have not been negotiated. Similarly, if a specific provision has not been negotiated between the parties, the nondrafting counsel need not advise the drafting attorney that the provision has not been drafted in a manner that is most favorable to the opposing party or advise the drafting attorney that he has failed to include a term that would be beneficial to his client. However, if a provision has been negotiated between the parties, the attorney must bring to the opposing attorney's attention a failure to include such provision or if the drafted provision does not reflect the negotiated agreement.

As the attorneys redraft the document and a series of exchanges of the redraft ensues, the question is to what extent counsel must make opposing counsel aware of changes that have been made to the drafted document. To the extent that changes affect the allocation of rights, duties, and privileges of the parties, an attorney who revises a draft and sends it to opposing counsel must note the changes made. If the attorney's practice is to send a redraft that tracks the changes made in red-line or otherwise, it is sufficient to do so with respect to all provisions. If the attorney generally sends a letter outlining the substantive changes, such communication is sufficient. It would rarely be sufficient to merely send a new draft with no indication of the changes made, particularly when the changes are substantive. To the extent that the terms of the contract relate to material facts, the failure to disclose changes violates the obligation of truthfulness. Additionally, if a scrivener's error is made and it changes the substantive terms of the agreement, it is incumbent on the attorney to bring such error to the attention of opposing counsel. Clearly, once a final document has been agreed to by the parties, an attorney is under an obligation to make no changes to that document prior to signing.

3. Communications with Unrepresented Parties

To the extent that a party to a transaction is unrepresented, the attorney representing an opposing party has a duty to make the same disclosures that the attorney would be required to make to an opposing counsel, as outlined in subsection (c)(2) above. However, throughout the process of drafting, negotiation, revision, and so forth, the attorney's duty to communicate information to unrepresented parties may be more extensive than the attorney's duty to communicate with the counsel of represented parties. As noted earlier in the portion of this text dealing with conflicts of interest, a lawyer is prohibited under Model Rule of Professional Conduct 4.3 from misleading an unrepresented participant as to whether the attorney is disinterested. It further imposes an obligation on the attorney to make a reasonable effort

---

**Drafting and Negotiation
Communicating with Counsel and Unrepresented Parties**

1. The attorney must advise opposing counsel and unrepresented parties of changes in the draft that impact the negotiated terms of the agreement.

2. The attorney must advise opposing counsel and unrepresented parties of a scrivener's error that changes the substance of the negotiated terms of the agreement.

3. Redrafts sent to opposing counsel and unrepresented parties should reflect the substantive changes made in the draft.

4. If unrepresented persons do not understand that the lawyer is acting only on behalf of her client the attorney must correct the misunderstanding.

5. Where an unrepresented person is unsophisticated and the terms of the transaction are one-sided in favor of the attorney's client, the attorney must not only communicate that the attorney represents the opposing party, but also must communicate the essentials of the drafted transaction.

6. The attorney may have a duty to advise third-party beneficiaries of the essentials of a drafted transaction.

---

to correct that misunderstanding if the attorney knows or has reason to know that such misunderstanding exists. Further, if the lawyer "knows or reasonably should know that the interests of such a person are or have a reasonable possibility of being in conflict with the interests of the client," the lawyer is prohibited from providing that person with legal advice, other than to advise that person to obtain independent legal counsel.[29] These duties exist at the outset of the process of formulating a deal, but also continue throughout that process. Thus, if an attorney is unaware that an unrepresented party misunderstands the attorney's representation at the beginning

---

29. MODEL RULES OF PROF'L CONDUCT R. 4.3 (2008).

of the transactional process but then becomes aware of it, that attorney has the same obligations to correct the misunderstanding and to avoid providing advice to such persons.

However, the duty of the attorney to various participants has been read even more broadly by the courts in some situations. Where the unrepresented person is unsophisticated and where the deal is extremely one-sided in favor of the attorney's client, the courts often impose an obligation upon the lawyer not only to apprise the unrepresented person of the lawyer's representation, but also to provide some minimal explanation of the terms of the deal. Additionally, where a third-party beneficiary is involved, courts will often impose similar requirements. In sum, the duty to unrepresented participants in the course of drafting, negotiations, and revision often includes a duty to explain to such participants the essential terms of the agreement.

INDEX

The NITA Foundation

supports NITA's core values of excellence, ethics, mentoring, inclusiveness, justice, and philanthropy through our various programs. We strive to give back to our global community by supporting the work of attorneys engaged in the representation of the underserved, indigent, and disenfranchised. To learn more about NITA's publications, programs, or the work of our Foundation, please visit us online at www.nitafoundation.org or by calling (877) 648-2632.

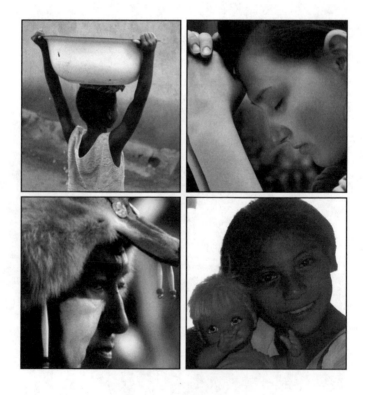

The NITA Foundation